MARK RAINSLEY

PADDLE THE WYE

A GUIDE FOR CANOES, KAYAKS AND SUPS

2nd Edition 2022

First published in under the title *River Wye Canoe and Kayak Guide* 2016

Published in Great Britain by Pesda Press
Tan y Coed Canol
Ceunant
Caernarfon
Gwynedd
LL55 4RN

Copyright © 2016 and 2022 Mark Rainsley

ISBN: 978-1-906095-87-1

The Author asserts the moral right to be identified as the author of this work.

All rights reserved. No part of this publication may be reproduced, stored in a retrieval system, or transmitted, in any form or by any means, electronic, mechanical, photocopying, recording or otherwise, without the prior written permission of the Publisher.

Printed and bound in Poland. www.hussarbooks.pl

Foreword

My first visit to the Wye, leading a group of young people, was an unforgettable experience; camping in the spectacular Symonds Yat gorge, swimming among huge brown trout, climbing Yat Rock, watching the kayaks looking like matchsticks on the river below, and kayaking through the rapids. It was to be the start of a long relationship with the River Wye; guiding and coaching, enjoying the water with family and friends, or just sitting on the bank watching the river go by.

Forty years on, in spite of pressure for regulation on our rivers, the essence of Wye life remains reassuringly familiar. Many thousands of people enjoy recreation in, on or beside the Wye every year, and we follow in the footsteps of those who have travelled the river, for sustenance, commerce or recreation, from time immemorial. From the numerous Wye guides and memoirs published over the years, we learn of Victorian ladies and gentlemen being rowed downriver to see the sights, while more energetic contemporaries tramp the route from source to sea or canoe the length of the river. This guidebook will help another generation of travellers to discover the River Wye. Have fun, and remember that the river is ours; never to exploit, but to explore, enjoy, care for, and safeguard for future generations of Wye travellers.

Pam Bell

WATERS OF WALES

WWW.WATERSOFWALES.ORG

Contents

Foreword 3
Contents 4
Introduction 6
About the author 7
Acknowledgements 8
Disclaimer 9

The River Wye 11
An overview of the Wye 11
Climate and flows 12
Launching on the Wye 12

Planning your Journey 15
Who? 15
Which Paddlecraft? 15
Canoe hire 17
Carrying gear 18
Safety 18
Water levels 22
Expedition itineraries 24
Duke of Edinburgh's Award expeditions 27
Ordnance Survey maps 29

The Upper Wye – Plynlimon to Glasbury 32
Plynlimon 35
Section 1 – Pont Rhydgaled to Pont Llangurig 41
Section 2 – Pont Llangurig to Rhayader 45
Section 3 – Rhayader to Newbridge-on-Wye 51
Section 4 – Newbridge-on-Wye to Builth Wells 57
Section 5 – Builth Wells to Erwood 61
Section 6 – Erwood to Glasbury 67

The Middle Wye – Glasbury to Ross-on-Wye 70
Section 7 – Glasbury to Whitney Bridge 73
Section 8 – Whitney Bridge to Bycross 79
Section 9 – Bycross to Hereford 85
Section 10 – Hereford to Hoarwithy 91
Section 11 – Hoarwithy to Ross-on-Wye 99

The Lower Wye – Ross-on-Wye to Chepstow 105
Section 12 – Ross-on-Wye to Symonds Yat East 107
Section 13 – Symonds Yat East to Monmouth 115
Section 14 – Monmouth to Brockweir 123
Section 15 – Brockweir to Chepstow 129
The Mouth of the Wye 137

Access 143
Middle Wye and Lower Wye 143
Upper Wye 143
Responsibilities 144
Further information 145

Camping 146

Wildlife and Environment 153
Environmental issues 153
Wildlife 155

Culture and Landscape: The Story of the Wye 161
Geology 161
History 164

Other Activities 168
Paddlesports 168
Walking 168
Mountain biking 169
Climbing 169

Code of Conduct 170

Further Information 172
Tourist information 172
Useful books 172
Historical sources 172

Index 173

Introduction

How oft, in spirit, have I turned to thee,
O sylvan Wye! Thou wanderer thro' the woods,
How often has my spirit turned to thee!
William Wordsworth, 'Lines Composed a Few Miles above Tintern Abbey' 1798

The River Wye is Britain's finest paddlesport touring river. There now, I've said it. What makes it so fine? Well, it has something for every kind of river paddler, from those seeking whitewater excitement to those favouring sedate cruising. The Wye is unusual in that it flows freely, without dams or weirs to interrupt its flow. Most of the river has sufficient water to paddle year-round, providing opportunities for a variety of day-long adventures and multi-day expeditions. The scenery along its 252 kilometres is never less than fine and is often spectacular, encompassing a wide range of environments from the mountains of Mid Wales, the hills and plains of Herefordshire, limestone gorges and the tidal reaches approaching the Severn Estuary. The wildlife is another draw, being diverse (from ancient woodlands and otters, to red kites and water crowfoot), and easy to encounter from your paddlecraft.

Paddling the Wye becomes even more enjoyable as you learn about its dimensions beyond the natural surrounds. History is writ large along the banks, from prehistoric hillforts, medieval castles and monasteries to – surprisingly – glimpses of the Industrial Revolution, which originated here. Through the remarkable Wye Tour, the river became the birthplace of package tourism and tourist guidebooks. Eighteenth and nineteenth-century artists participated in this adventure and left a huge legacy of travelogues, poems and paintings. Paddlers enjoying these today get to appreciate the Wye from a wider perspective; some excerpts are included here as they still offer useful information.

This is the first paddling guidebook to the River Wye which covers the entire river in all its moods, which offers detailed advice on planning trips and expeditions, and which explores the Wye's splendid wildlife, landscape, history and culture. I hope it helps you to enjoy many great adventures on this fine river.

Mark Rainsley

About the author

Mark Rainsley

Mark has spent over three decades using paddlesport as a means of avoiding adulthood and responsibility. He is a fanatical paddler who has descended challenging whitewater rivers worldwide, and who is dedicated to exploring every nook and cranny of the UK's coast and rivers by canoe and kayak. He is a prolific contributor to paddlesport magazines and other media. Mark has authored numerous other Pesda Press guidebooks including *South West Sea Kayaking, Paddle Shakespeare's Avon, Paddle the Severn* and *Paddle the Thames*.

Mark's earliest experience of paddlesport was on regular family holidays to the River Wye in the 1970s. He floundered around in a barge-like fibreglass kayak, which his dad also used to terrify the family by carrying out a death-defying impromptu descent of the Symonds Yat rapids. In more recent times, Mark has become a parent himself and has relished introducing his daughter to paddlesport via canoe expeditions on the River Wye.

Mark at Symonds Yat, 1980.

Acknowledgements

Many thanks to all those friends and family who joined me during research for this guidebook. While paddling the wonderful Wye was hardly a hardship for them, tolerating my agenda and being bossed around for photographic purposes probably was! Special thanks to my favourite paddling companions; my lovely wife Heather and my gorgeous daughter Ellen.

The following folk provided expert input. Pam Bell was kind enough to write the foreword, as well as offering experienced input to the Access section. Wye Valley Area of Outstanding Natural Beauty (AONB) Officer Andrew Blake generously allowed us to reproduce their *Code of Conduct for Canoeists on the Wye*. Jane Hughes of Wye Valley Canoes provided useful perspectives from the hire and guiding industry. Grace Payne-James supplied a fun account of her Duke of Edinburgh expedition experiences on the Wye, and Dr Lizzie Garnett checked over the geology section.

Finally, thanks to Franco Ferrero and his team at Pesda Press, and Don Williams of Bute Cartographics.

Photographs

All photographs by Mark Rainsley, except where acknowledged in the captions.

◎ *Below Bigsweir Bridge.*

Important notice – disclaimer

Paddlesports, whether in a river or sea environment, have their inherent risks, as do all adventurous activities. This guidebook highlights some considerations to take into account when planning your own river journey.

While we have included a range of factors to consider, you will need to plan your own journey, and within that ensure there is scope to be adaptable to local conditions; for example tides, weather and ever-changing river hazards. This requires knowing your own abilities, then applying your own risk assessment to the conditions that you may encounter. The varying environmental conditions along the River Wye mean that everyday good judgement is required to decide whether to paddle or not.

The information within this book has been well researched. However, neither the author nor Pesda Press can be held responsible for any decision about whether to paddle or not, and any consequences arising from that decision.

Coldwell Rocks, Lower Wye.

The River Wye

"It flows in a gentle, uninterrupted stream, and adorns, through its various reaches, a succession of the most picturesque scenes. The beauty of these scenes arises from ... the lofty banks of the river, and its mazy course."

William Gilpin, *Observations on the River Wye* 1783

An overview of the Wye

The River Wye is Britain's fifth longest river. It measures 252km from its source in the Cambrian Mountains to its mouth, where it empties into the Severn Estuary. It has a strong case to be Britain's most free-flowing major river; apart from a small gauging weir near the source and some fish steps at Rhayader, there are now no artificial weirs or dams.

The Wye is both a Welsh and an English river; it originates in Mid Wales, crosses into Herefordshire and then winds back towards Wales, at times forming the border. The Welsh name is *Afon Gwy*, possibly derived from *gwyr* or *gwybiol* (Old Welsh) meaning crooked or wandering hills.

In this guidebook, the river has been divided into three sections, reflecting the distinctive character of each.

The Upper Wye

The Upper Wye (*Gwy Uchaf*) is entirely Welsh. The river emerges high on Plynlimon Mountain, an exploration of which is recommended as a boggy walking day! The Wye quickly accumulates volume and power, flowing southwards through a series of steep-sided valleys. This is a whitewater river, with rapids up to grade 4; in other words, the paddling is quite challenging. Paddlers will need to utilise appropriate equipment and training. Water levels fluctuate quickly, with significant rises after rain or snowmelt. There is rarely sufficient flow for paddlers outside the winter and spring months. When there are good flows here, the Middle and Lower Wye might well be too high for comfort; hence, most will tackle the Upper Wye in isolation. The Cambrian Mountain scenery is wonderful, and this environment is home to a wide range of attractive and important flora and fauna.

The Middle Wye

The Middle Wye (*Gwy Ganol*) is characterised by looping meanders across a wide plain. The river leaves the mountains at Llyswen, spreading onto the Herefordshire Plain ... although Herefordshire itself (and England) is not reached until Hay-on-Wye. At this point, the river has already accumulated 53% of its final flow, and the River Lugg adds another 20% of this. The Middle Wye offers wonderful relaxed touring paddling, past riverbanks lined by woodland and farmland, as the river slowly winds from one hilly side of the plain to another. Below Hereford, the Wye AONB (Area of Outstanding Natural Beauty) is entered.

The Lower Wye

The Lower Wye (*Gwy Isaf*) is surprising. After Ross-on-Wye, the river is mature and seemingly sedate, with only the River Monnow remaining to contribute 8% of the flow at Monmouth. However it undergoes another significant change of character. It cuts two successive deep gorges through limestone hills, and is forced into sharp meanders by these hard barriers. The first gorge is around Symonds Yat, the second is found approaching Chepstow on the final stretch to the sea. Paddlers will encounter distinct but easy rapids in deep wooded vales, alongside a plethora of historical sites. The final reaches have the additional challenge of being tidal.

Needless to say, the scenery is often breathtaking; it is after all an AONB!

Climate and flows

The Wye has the fourth largest flow of any river in England and Wales. It drains 4,136 square kilometres and annually discharges about 2,500 million cubic metres of water at its mouth. The mean flow above Bigsweir (the tidal limit) is 73 cumecs (cubic metres a second). The Wye is almost never short of water. Along the Upper Wye in the Cambrian Mountains, over 2,000mm of rain falls annually, spread over more than 200 days. On the Middle Wye around Hereford it's rather drier with 665mm over 115 days. However, the uplands around the Lower Wye make for a wetter climate again with 1,020mm falling annually, spread across up to 200 days.

Launching on the Wye

The Wye has a reasonable number of spots, spread along its length, from which to launch your paddlecraft. The river sections in this book are designed to start and finish at launch points where accessing the water is reasonably simple (or is the least difficult of various options!). The list below is by no means exhaustive, but hopefully offers a wide enough range of possibilities to give access to all sections. Many charge for parking and some charge launching fees. It should be noted that not all spots listed are on public land; check details in the section description.

Waypoint	Grid reference	Post code	Possible launch point?	Distance from previous waypoint	Distance from the source of the Wye	Distance from Glasbury
Upper Wye						
Source of the Wye	SN 802 872				0km	
Pont Rhydgaled	SN 841 827	SY18 6SY	Y, RL	7.2km	7.2km	
Pont Llangurig	SN 908 797	SY18 6SG	Y, RL	9.8km	17km	
Dolhelfa	SN 921 738	SY18 6RY	Y, RR	7km	24km	
Pont Marteg	SN 951 716	LD6 5LE	Y, RL	4.3km	28.3km	
Rhayader	SN 969 677	LD6 5AL	Y. RL	5.2km	33.5km	
Llanwrthwl Bridge	SN 976 640	LD1 6NS	Y, RL	5.9km	39.4km	
Newbridge	SO 014 583	LD1 6LY	Y, RR	8.8km	48.2km	
Builth Wells	SO 042 511	LD2 3DW	Y, RR	11.3km	59.5km	
Erwood	SO 105 428	LD2 3SZ	Y, RL	13.8km	73.3km	
Boughrood Bridge	SO 130 384	LD3 0YB	Y, RR	5.2km	78.5km	
Middle Wye						
Glasbury Bridge	SO 179 392	HR3 5NW	Y, RL	6.7km	85.2km	0km
Hay-on-Wye	SO 229 427	HR3 5BJ	Y, RR	9.3km	94.5km	9.3km
Whitney Bridge	SO 259 475	HR3 6EW	Y, RL	7.4km	101.9km	16.7km
Whitney-on-Wye	SO 269 472	HR3 6EH	Y, RL	1km	102.9km	17.7km
Brewardine Bridge	SO 336 447	HR3 6BT	Y, RR	13.4km	116.3km	31.1km
Byecross Farm	SO 376 436	HR2 9LJ	y	6.3km	122.6km	37.4km
Byford	SO 400 425	HR4 7LD	Y, RL	3.4km	126km	40.8km
Hereford Rowing Club	SO 506 395	HR4 0BE	Y, RL	16km	142km	56.8km
Hereford	SO 509 396	HR4 9DW	Y, RR	0.3km	142.3km	57.1km
Lucksall Caravan and Camping Park	SO 568 363	HR1 4LP	Y, RL	11.9km	154.2km	69km
Hoarwithy	SO 548 292	HR2 6QH	Y, RL/ RR	13.4km	167.6km	82.4km
Lower Wye						
Ross-on-Wye	SO 595 241	HR9 7BT	Y, RL	18.8km	186.4km	101.2km
Kerne Bridge	SO 582 187	HR9 5QT	Y, RL	9.7km	196.1km	110.9km
Lower Lydbrook	SO 596 170	GL17 9NJ	Y, RL	3.5km	199.6km	114.4km
Huntsham Bridge Camping	SO 568 181	HR9 6JN	Y, RL	6.7km	206.3km	121.1km
Symonds Yat West	SO 557 165	HR9 6BN	Y, RR	3km	209.3km	124.1km
Symonds Yat East	SO 561 160	HR9 6BY	Y, RL	0.5km	209.8km	124.6km
Monmouth	SO 512 129	NP25 3SH	Y, RR	8.4km	218.2km	133km
Brockweir	SO 539 012	NP16 7NG	Y, RL	15.2km	233.4km	148.2km
Chepstow	ST 537 942	NP16 5HH	Y, RR	14.1km	247.5km	162.3km
Chapel Rock	ST 548 900		N	5km	252.5km	167.3km
Beachley Landing Pier	ST 552 907	NP16 7HH	Y	0.8km	253.3km	168.1km

Tintern mooring

Planning your Journey

Whether you plan a day trip in hired canoes or a multi-day expedition, planning can make all the difference to your Wye adventure. Selecting the correct equipment, checking the river levels and choosing the right challenge for your group will help make your journey an enjoyable and successful experience.

Who?

This is simple; the Wye is suitable for and accessible to all ages, genders and abilities. Complete beginners or novices on the Middle and Lower Wye will find a perfect environment for learning and progressing quickly, provided they plan appropriately. The Upper Wye is different, being suited to those who are experienced, or developing their skills, at whitewater paddling.

Which paddlecraft?

Canoes are open-topped craft within which one or more paddlers sit or kneel, propelling themselves with single-bladed paddles. They are also known as 'open canoes' or 'Canadian canoes'. Kayaks can have closed decks or open decks (known as 'sit-on-tops' or SOTs) but the key difference is that the paddler sits, propelling him- or herself with a two-bladed paddle. Some kayaks have seats for more than

Children love the Wye too.

Kayaks.

Inflatable kayak.

Wild swimming.

one paddler. Just to complicate and confuse things, in Britain it is normal to use the word `canoe' to refer to both canoes and kayaks!

Stand-up paddleboards (SUPs) are ubiquitous, now possibly outnumbering canoes and kayaks on the water. Their huge popularity (with a notable bias towards female participation) is partly explained by their accessibility (stand up, paddle) but also by the pure pleasure of traveling in this simple way, with an elevated viewpoint and your whole bodies' musculature actively involved, despite minimal connection to the craft. They are now commonly used for long trips and even multi-day expeditions. If shopping for a paddleboard, look for a model with a bit of length (10' 6" at least) for touring and decent deck elastics for carrying gear!

Which is best for the Wye? All are great. Canoes carry far more food and equipment, and are quicker to learn how to handle than kayaks. Kayaks are more manoeuvrable and less affected by wind, while paddleboards can be mastered quite quickly but are hard work in wind and limited in gear capacity. Paddleboards can struggle with shallow rapids, if their skegs are too long.

Other kinds of paddlecraft are of course available. Inflatable kayaks are for example common, a hybrid of raft and kayak. They are easy to transport off the water (onto trains and so forth) but slow and susceptible to the wind.

The following books are recommended if you want to learn more about selecting and handling paddlecraft:

Canoeing, Ray Goodwin, Pesda Press, 2016, ISBN 978 1906095543

Sit-on-top Kayak, Derek Hairon, Pesda Press, 2007, ISBN 978 1906095024

Stand up paddleboard.

Canoe hire

The canoe hire industry is well established all along the Middle and Lower Wye, with numerous companies offering equipment hire, guiding and coaching. Usually they also offer river advice, and a shuttle service to return you to the start of your trip.

Enjoying hired canoes and equipment.

Advice from a hire company

"There are a lot of canoe hire companies along the Wye where you can hire canoes, kayaks or double kayaks for anything from a half day to a five day paddling trip.

Look for a company that is either AALA licensed (Adventure Activity Licensing Authority) or part of the BCU Paddlesport Provider Scheme, as they will be monitored for giving sound safety advice and reliable equipment. Talk to them about your group and your needs. All companies should give you a map, a safety briefing and paddling advice before you set out. If you are taking children, we recommend that you have done the stretch before or had some previous paddling experience. If you are new to paddling and in doubt about your ability, ask for an instructor or a guide for your first trip, especially if you have children. You paddle downstream and when you reach your destination the hire company will come and collect you and your canoe and take you back to the start.

Most of the time, the Wye is at a great level for beginners canoeing, but should never be undertaken when the river levels are high or significantly rising. So, if there has been persistent heavy rain in Mid Wales before your trip it is definitely worth checking, not only with the hire company, but also on the Environment Agency and the Natural Resources Wales websites to see what the river is doing.

Take a phone, some warm clothes in case anyone capsizes or gets cold, some sun cream and a hat in warm weather, and a bit of food and soft drink in a waterproof container or barrel.

There really is no better way to spend some time with family or friends, so finally I would say enjoy the journey rather than just power on to your destination; look out for the wildlife, take time to relax, to chat and to slow down for a few hours or a few days."

Jane Hughes, Wye Valley Canoes, Glasbury
www.wyevalleycanoes.co.uk

📷 Blue barrel for packing.

Carrying gear

Whether you are travelling for a day or a week, your equipment will need protecting and waterproofing. Sodden dinner followed by a sodden sleeping bag in a sodden tent is no fun!* Hire companies often loan watertight plastic barrels for use in canoes, which helpfully keep large amounts of gear dry and protected from knocks. A recent innovation is waterproof 60-litre duffle bags, with a rolldown closure along the length of the bag; these are cheap and fit better in the canoe, but are not 100% dry if submerged. For kayaks and paddleboards, the best option is to use small and flexible `drybags' which are sealed by a roll-top closure. These fit down the back of most kayaks, with a little persuasion. Unless you buy very expensive designs, dry bags are still likely to allow some water in; consider putting your kit in thick plastic bags inside the dry bags. Camera equipment and other fragile expensive equipment should ideally be protected in solid cases with padding, such as those produced by Peli Products. Barrels, dry bags and solid cases will all result in soaking

📷 Loaded canoe.

or destroyed kit if you forget to close and seal them properly.

Safety

This section is about *safety*; enabling paddlers to select appropriate equipment and to understand hazards encountered on the Wye, to avoid getting into difficulty.

Don't be alarmed! In normal summer water levels, the River Wye is a relatively forgiving and safe environment which is suited to

*Actual author experience.

novices and the inexperienced, if a little common sense is applied in planning, selecting equipment and avoiding hazards. There are important exceptions to this rule however:

- The Upper Wye is a true whitewater river, paddled mostly in the colder months. The hazards described below are much less forgiving on the Upper, which is only suited to those with appropriate skills and experience.
- The Lower Wye below Bigsweir Bridge is a tidal river, with the Bristol Channel's huge tidal range causing strong currents and making the banks inaccessible due to expanses of deep mud. Only venture here if you are confident and experienced in tidal waters. The river below Chepstow is particularly hazardous.
- All bets are off if the water level is high; this exacerbates all of the normal hazards, making them harder to avoid and much more consequential.

Paddlers who want to learn more about the subject of safety (and rescue) are recommended to seek specialist training, or to consult *White Water Safety and Rescue* by Franco Ferrero (Pesda Press, 2006, ISBN 9780954706159).

Clothing and equipment
Flotation
Whichever craft you choose to float down the Wye, it must have some form of fixed buoyancy to prevent it from sinking when waterlogged. This is usually achieved through inflatable air bags, solid foam or sealed chambers in the boat.

Entrapment hazards
Make sure that any ropes, straps or suchlike are securely stowed away and cannot form a loop or point of entrapment/snagging for a paddler's foot or hand.

Why you need fixed bouyancy.

Safe clothing for the Upper Wye.

Buoyancy aids

A well-fitted buoyancy aid is essential, and will make a swim much less dangerous. On calm and slow-moving parts of the river in summer, experienced adult paddlers who are strong swimmers may make a personal choice to remove it; if so, it should always be quickly available to hand.

Clothing

Your clothing needs to protect you from becoming hypothermic by remaining warm when wet and by providing a shield from the wind. Wetsuits do this well, but will probably be over-warm and restrictive in summer. An ideal solution might be to wear polypropylene or fleece thermals with a cagoule on top. Legs need similar protection, and don't forget a warm hat for your head! Helmets also retain heat well, and may be a good idea for young or inexperienced paddlers on the Middle and Lower Wye; on the Upper they are essential. Footwear should offer protection when scrambling ashore on muddy banks. You should also carry spare dry clothing.

Sun protection

Waterproof sun cream and a brimmed hat will protect your skin and save you from the prospect of having to paddle with painful, chafing sunburn on the following day.

Phones

A mobile phone (packed in a waterproof container) is useful for summoning assistance in an emergency. Phone reception is of course variable in the winding valleys of the Wye.

River hazards
Trees and bushes

Tree branches and bushes always lurk in the water along the riverbanks. Usually these 'strainers' are simple to avoid, however rivers flow towards the outsides of bends, and erode back the banks; as a result you can find yourself being drawn towards or beneath overhanging foliage; steer to avoid. Occasionally, whole trees fall into the river, forming natural sieves; totally avoid!

Tree hazard.

Bridges

Be careful when approaching the Wye's bridges, as the current piles onto the upstream side of the bridge pillars. Some are designed to smoothly redirect water (and paddlers?) but regardless, steer well clear. Sometimes tree branches and other junk pile up on the pillars, causing a significant hazard.

Bridge pillar.

Rocks and shallows

Rocks in the riverbed usually present few problems on the Middle and Lower Wye. The only risk is grounding on shallow spots during the summer months. Avoid this by keeping your boat pointing downstream and by recognising the V-shape of deep water which flows between shallow spots ... this is where you want to aim!

Waves and stoppers

Waves on the Middle and Lower Wye's rapids are unlikely to be large enough to do more than splash you, and most often present themselves as mere riffles. It might however be possible to swamp an open canoe on the Symonds Yat rapids, if you tried enough times! Stoppers are waves which fold back on themselves below drops, 'stopping' or even holding paddlers. These are uncommon below Glasbury, the only noticeable ones forming below small rocks at Symonds Yat. Man-made weirs form dangerous stoppers, but (other than some fish steps at Rhayader) there are no weirs on the Wye.

Wind

If you have a forecast of very strong winds, you may wish to adjust your plans. These can make kayaks and (especially) canoes and paddleboards difficult to steer, or even unmanageable. On long straight sections, the wind can whip up small steep waves, especially when the wind is blowing against the flow. The prevailing winds come from the south-west.

Waves at Symonds Yat. Photo | Lucy Perry.

Other craft

Steer clear of rowers at Hereford, Ross-on-Wye and Monmouth; they will have their backs to you! Two slow tour boats operate from Symonds Yat West, but otherwise there are no powered boats. Note however that fast powered boats are common on the tidal Wye around Chepstow.

Seeking help

If you find yourself in serious difficulty and in need of assistance, then do not hesitate to call the UK emergency phone number 999. Give details of your group, your difficulty and perhaps most importantly; your location. The operator will summon the Police, Ambulance, Fire Service, Mountain Rescue, Lowland Rescue or Coastguard as appropriate.

SARA

The Severn Area Rescue Association is the UK's second largest lifeboat service and covers the Severn Estuary, in place of the RNLI. They have a station beneath the Severn Bridge at Beachley, and it is their volunteer crew and RIBs (inflatables) that would be tasked to deal with any emergency on the tidal Wye. Further info from www.sara-rescue.org.uk.

Water levels

It's surprisingly hard to ascertain the level of the Wye before setting off to paddle. Information on river levels is available from the Environment Agency, https://flood-warning-information.service.gov.uk/river-and-sea-levels and via their automated telephone service (0906 6197755, premium rate). The website

High water conditions at Penddol Rocks on the Upper Wye.

gives readouts from numerous gauging stations along the Wye and its tributaries. However, looking at their graphs, you'll realise that the data is actually quite unhelpful. The system is set up to warn of floods, and little else; major changes are needed in the river's flow before the graphs noticeably alter. Hence, paddlers have to use their judgement and common sense. For the Upper Wye, assume that the river will usually only be paddleable in winter and spring, and even then may be low and scrapey unless there has been rain or snowmelt in recent days. The Middle and Lower Wye will be paddleable year-round; even in severe drought, compensatory water will be added from the Elan Valley reservoirs. If you arrive and find only minimal amounts of beach or gravel bars showing, assume that the river is flowing high and take appropriate care. If none are showing, the river is very high and you should re-think your plans. Of course, it is tricky for those unfamiliar with the river to make this judgement; a good idea if unsure is to seek advice from hire centres and suchlike. The water level can suddenly change significantly year-round, with a one to three-day lag before heavy rain in the Cambrian Mountains finds its way downstream to the Middle and Lower Wye. Drag your boat up high and remember to tie it up overnight!

A flood run

A group of experienced whitewater kayakers including the author attempted to paddle from Glasbury to Chepstow over two days, when the river was on Environment Agency flood alert. The Wye was three to four metres higher than normal, and barely remained within its banks. At first, we managed to keep in the centre of the flow and avoid the submerged trees, bushes and fences lining the banks. We covered 45 miles in five hours! However, finding places to stop safely was a challenge, and we encountered an unforeseen hazard; wind. Storm force blasts made us struggle to hold onto our paddles, let alone paddle in control. Approaching the River Lugg, we encountered a vast lake spanning the floodplain. We were confused; we'd assumed that – paddling downstream faster than the river's flow – we would keep ahead of rising water levels. Of course, tributaries such as the Lugg can add to and even 'back up' the flow of the Wye. It was now hard to discern the Wye from farmland. We were lucky to have made it this far, and were clearly no longer in control. We pulled ashore at the first opportunity (the middle of someone's garden, miles downstream) and bailed on our foolish venture.

Expedition itineraries

This book's guides to sections of the Wye are of course paddling trip itineraries, each lasting from half a day to a day. Outlined below are ideas for joining these into multi-day expeditions.

The Upper Wye offers nearly 80km of white-water paddling above Glasbury. Below Glasbury, it is over 160km along the Middle and Lower Wye to Chepstow, just before the Severn Estuary is reached. A wide variety of multi-day expeditions are possible along the Wye's length, a selection of which is suggested here. The itineraries are based around the locations of riverside campsites, although not all are available at all times; check before setting off! The 'easy' touring expeditions cover around 20km a day, achievable by anyone and allowing time to stop and explore sights en route. The 'medium' tours cover around 30km a day, which for most will mean full days of paddling. The 'hard' tours take on around 40km a day; achieving these distances at typical summer water levels will require a head-down paddling approach, leaving little time for tourism. Whichever itinerary you decide upon, the good news is ... it's all good. There are absolutely no duff stretches on this wonderful river.

Touring expeditions

Five-day trip – easy

Day	From	To	Distance (km)
1	Byecross Farm	Hereford	19.7
2	Hereford	Hoarwithy	25.3
3	Hoarwithy	Ross-on-Wye	18.8
4	Ross-on-Wye	Symonds Yat East	23.4
5	Symonds Yat East	Monmouth/ Brockweir	8.9 / 23.6

Five-day trip – medium

Day	From	To	Distance (km)
1	Hay-on-Wye	Byecross Farm	28.1
2	Byecross Farm	Lucksall Caravan & Camping Park	31.6
3	Lucksall Caravan & Camping Park	Ross-on-Wye	32.2
4	Ross-on-Wye	Monmouth	31.8
5	Monmouth	Chepstow	29.3

Five-day trip – hard

Day	From	To	Distance (km)
1	Glasbury	Oakfield Farm	19.7
2	Oakfield Farm	Hereford	37.4
3	Hereford	Foy	38.0
4	Foy	Symonds Yat East	29.5
5	Symonds Yat East	Chepstow	37.7

Four-day trip – easy

Day	From	To	Distance (km)
1	Glasbury	Whitney Bridge	16.7
2	Whitney Bridge	Byecross Farm	20.7
3	Byecross Farm	Hereford	19.7
4	Hereford	Lucksall Caravan & Camping Park / Hoarwithy	11.9 / 25.3

Three-day trip – easy

Day	From	To	Distance (km)
1	Lucksall Caravan & Camping Park	Hoarwithy	13.4
2	Hoarwithy	Ross-on-Wye	18.8
3	Ross-on-Wye	Symonds Yat East	23.4

Four-day trip – medium

Day	From	To	Distance (km)
1	Hay-on-Wye	Byecross Farm	28.1
2	Byecross Farm	Lucksall Caravan & Camping Park	31.6
3	Lucksall Caravan & Camping Park	Ross-on-Wye	32.2
4	Ross-on-Wye	Ross-on-Wye	31.8

Three-day trip – medium

Day	From	To	Distance (km)
1	Hay-on-Wye	Byecross Farm	28.1
2	Byecross Farm	Lucksall Caravan & Camping Park	31.6
3	Lucksall Caravan & Camping Park	Ross-on-Wye	32.2

Four-day trip – hard

Day	From	To	Distance (km)
1	Glasbury	Byecross Farm	37.4
2	Byecross Farm	Hoarwithy	45
3	Hoarwithy	Symonds Yat East	42.2
4	Symonds Yat East	Chepstow	37.7

Three-day trip – hard

Day	From	To	Distance (km)
1	Byford	Hoarwithy	41.6
2	Hoarwithy	Symonds Yat East	42.2
3	Symonds Yat East	Chepstow	37.7

Whitewater expeditions

The Upper Wye has good potential for multi-day whitewater paddling, but this is most likely to be practical in the colder months when camping is uncomfortable ... and in any case, there are few camping options! The suggestions here utilise places where B&B and suchlike accommodation is available.

Rhayader Town Falls on the Upper Wye.

Source to the Plains expedition
Grade 2 to 4

This would be a marvellous adventure, but would need planning to coordinate the paddle down to Rhayader with recent rain. This would best suit specialist whitewater canoes (OC1s) or whitewater kayaks.

Grade 2 and 3 expedition

This avoids long sections of technical rapids, leaving just a few notable grade 3 rapids to paddle or portage. Expedition-rigged touring canoes (with flotation!) would be in their element here.

Day	From	To	Distance (km)
1	Walk Plynlimon?		12
2	Pont Rhydgaled	Rhayader	26.3
3	Rhayader	Builth Wells	26
4	Builth Wells	Glasbury	25.7
5	Glasbury	Hay-on-Wye	9.3

Day	From	To	Distance (km)
1	Walk Plynlimon?		12
2	Llanwrthwl Bridge	Builth Wells	20.1
3	Builth Wells	Boughrood Bridge	19
4	Boughrood Bridge	Whitney Bridge	23.4

Luke Hughes

However challenging and epic your Wye expedition might be, it almost certainly pales into insignificance next to the efforts of 18th-century innkeeper Luke Hughes. In the 1730s, Hughes made a bet that he could paddle a tiny coracle from his inn at Wilton (near Ross-on-Wye) downriver to the Severn estuary, then along the Bristol Channel and out to the island of Lundy, twenty miles offshore ... and back again. Incredibly he completed his feat, returning after two weeks to a hero's welcome at Wilton.

Duke of Edinburgh's Award expeditions

The Duke of Edinburgh's Awards for 14–24 year olds are intended to *"inspire, guide and support young people in their self-development"*. A key component of the awards is *"To inspire young people to develop initiative and a spirit of adventure and discovery, by planning, training for and completing an adventurous self-sufficient journey, as part of a team."*

The Middle and Lower Wye are popular with DofE expedition groups. Various sections (or indeed the whole) can be utilised for expedition training or for final qualifying expeditions. The river flows through areas fitting the DofE's definitions of 'rural' and 'wild country'. There is an undisputed right of navigation. Riverside campsites are available at convenient intervals. Equipment and guides/instructors are simple to find and hire. It is easy for a DofE supervisor to unobtrusively monitor a group's progress at bridges and viewpoints. The river is almost purpose-made for DofE!

DofE requirements for 'canoeing and rowing' expeditions

Selecting a section of the Wye which meets the relevant award criteria (overleaf) is straightforward. The less wild river around Hereford might suit as a Bronze Award environment, while a Gold Award expedition could take large parts of the Middle and Lower Wye, perhaps including the tidal reaches to Chepstow. The Wye also has excellent potential for selecting engaging and challenging expedition aims; the wildlife and environment are easy to access and observe, while the region's amazing history offers more

Duke of Edinburgh group at Byecross Farm.

ideas. Why not investigate the legacy of the Wye Tour, for example?

The Severn and Wye Expedition Network can offer further guidance, and have a fleet of canoes and trailer available for hire by groups: Severn and Wye Expedition Network, The Duke of Edinburgh's Award, 1st Floor Offices, Arthur House, 21 Mere Green Road, Sutton Coldfield, Birmingham B75 5BL. Further advice on DofE expeditions on water can also be found in Chapter 13 of the *Expedition Guide*.

The DofE Award Expedition Guide, Alex Davies, The Award Scheme Ltd., 2019, ISBN 9780905425207

Award	Recommended environment	Duration of expedition	Advised distances (km)
Bronze	Canals, rivers or other inland waterways & lakes. The water and area may be familiar to participants.	2 days, 1 night, 6 hours of planned activity daily	16–20 daily, 32–40 total
Silver	Canals, rivers or other inland waterways and lakes in rural areas. The water must be unfamiliar to the participants and present an appropriate challenge. There is an expectation that the conditions will be related to the age and experience of the participants and represent a progression between Bronze and Gold.	3 days, 2 nights, 7 hours of planned activity daily	22km daily, 65km total
Gold	Rivers or other inland waterways and lakes in rural areas, sheltered coastal waters or estuaries. The water must be unfamiliar to the participants and must present an appropriate challenge. At Gold level routes should be in or pass through wild country. Moving water, either by current or tide, or large bodies of water, should be sought where possible.	4 days, 3 nights, 8 hours of planned activity daily	32km daily, 128km total

Which bank?

Throughout this book, the terms 'river left' and 'river right' are commonly used to locate features. 'River left' is simply the left hand bank *when you are looking downstream*, and 'river right' is ... okay, you get it.

River left and ...   ... river right.

Ordnance Survey maps

Section	1:50000 Landranger map(s)	1:25000 Explorer map(s)
Plynlimon	135, 136	213, 214
1	136	214
2	136, 147	200, 214
3	136, 147	200
4	147	188, 200
5	147, 148, 161	188
6	147, 148, 161	188
7	148, 161	188, 201
8	148, 149, 161	201
9	148, 149, 161	189, 201, 202
10	149	189
11	149, 162	OL14, 189
12	162	OL14, 189
13	162	OL14
14	162	OL14, 167
15	162	OL14, 167
Mouth of the Wye	162	OL14, 167

Grace's expedition

At Easter my friend Megan and I completed an 80 mile canoeing expedition on the River Wye. This was the practice part of our Gold Duke of Edinburgh's Award. We were in a group of four with two boys from another school. On a training day, we learned how to capsize safely and gained a feel of who was best being at the front, and who at the back – although it took us the majority of the day to be able to go in a straight line because we have terrible coordination! Nevertheless, once we'd got it sussed there was little that could stop us.

I had been warned that the Wye is a slow-moving river, and that we would be paddling continuously throughout the four days. However, in the week leading up to our expedition, we had 65mph winds and torrential rain. The river had risen, resulting in the Wye having a fantastic flow the entire way ... which none of us felt the need to complain about!

Our journey began in Glasbury where we learned to safely tie in our barrels and waterproof everything we owned, something we definitely needed to do considering the canoe was going to be similar to a bath tub, thanks to all the rain. Our expedition leader Chris made the executive decision to raft our two canoes together to give us more stability in these high water conditions.

The first day started well, we kept our spirits up by singing silly songs as we paddled. Well, Megan and I did, the boys weren't quite as impressed. The wind continued to pick up. Disaster struck as we turned the corner of one meander; the wind got the better of us and pushed us into the far bank. The more we fought, the more we were driven back until finally the back end of our canoe was pushed under by the iron grip of the water. We were tired, slowly sinking and not making any progress; all the while Chris was shouting at us to paddle harder! Eventually the wind let up enough for us to get off the bank. After that mishap, the day continued relatively problem-free and once we got to our checkpoint for lunch we enjoyed a comforting meal of Mug Shot pasta and beef jerky. We were able to reflect on how well we worked as a team to get out of that dicey situation.

We woke up the next morning hearing the pitter-patter of rain on the roof of the tent. The biggest challenge for all of us on this second day was the ache in our arms. We'd all anticipated it, but hadn't expected it to be quite so bad. With a little encouragement to each other and a regular regime of swapping arms, we were able to keep powering through to each checkpoint. On the third day we began to think about which project we would carry out on our final expedition in July. We chose to document the wildlife, after the hairy experience of being chased by very angry swans that happened to be fighting over a potential mate. Chris helped us practise spotting the different birds on the river and where to look for which types; for example herons tend to be up high, whereas geese will be on the banks. The Wye is rich in different species including peregrine falcons, although try as we might, we never did manage to spot one. Our final day was the most exciting because we had finally reached the Symonds Yat rapids. By this point we had derafted into two separate canoes. We had to aim for the correct point; otherwise we would have been going for a very cold dip! Chris rated us on accurate positioning for the canoe. Megan scored nine out of ten for choosing the right path, whereas I only achieved a six. Megan still ended up wetter out of the two of us – we don't know how that happened!

There wasn't far to go after the rapids, but there was beautiful scenery as we followed the meanders below Symonds Yat Rock. A goose took a particular interest in Megan and Peter's canoe; they got a lovely view of the inside of its mouth as it honked at them, scarier than you'd think!

After much laughter and a lot of rain we arrived at Monmouth to be greeted by our (very relieved) parents. The last thing was to unpack everything and load the canoes on the trailer, but by now we were a well-oiled machine and were finished in no time. The River Wye was a fantastic experience for us all. We were able to appreciate a totally new part of Britain which I for one had never seen before. It fully prepared us for our final expedition, thanks to the testing conditions we practised in.

Grace Payne-James

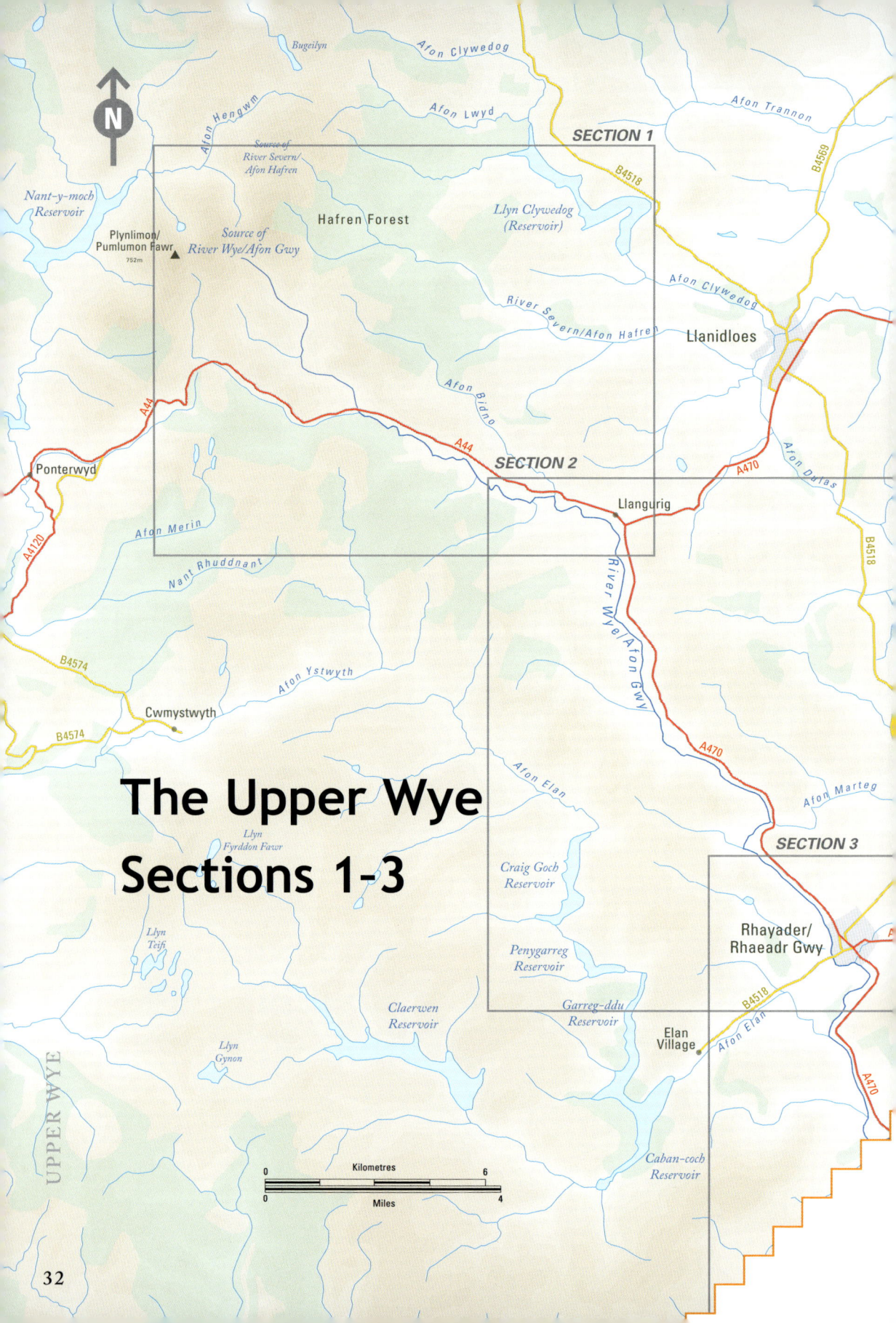

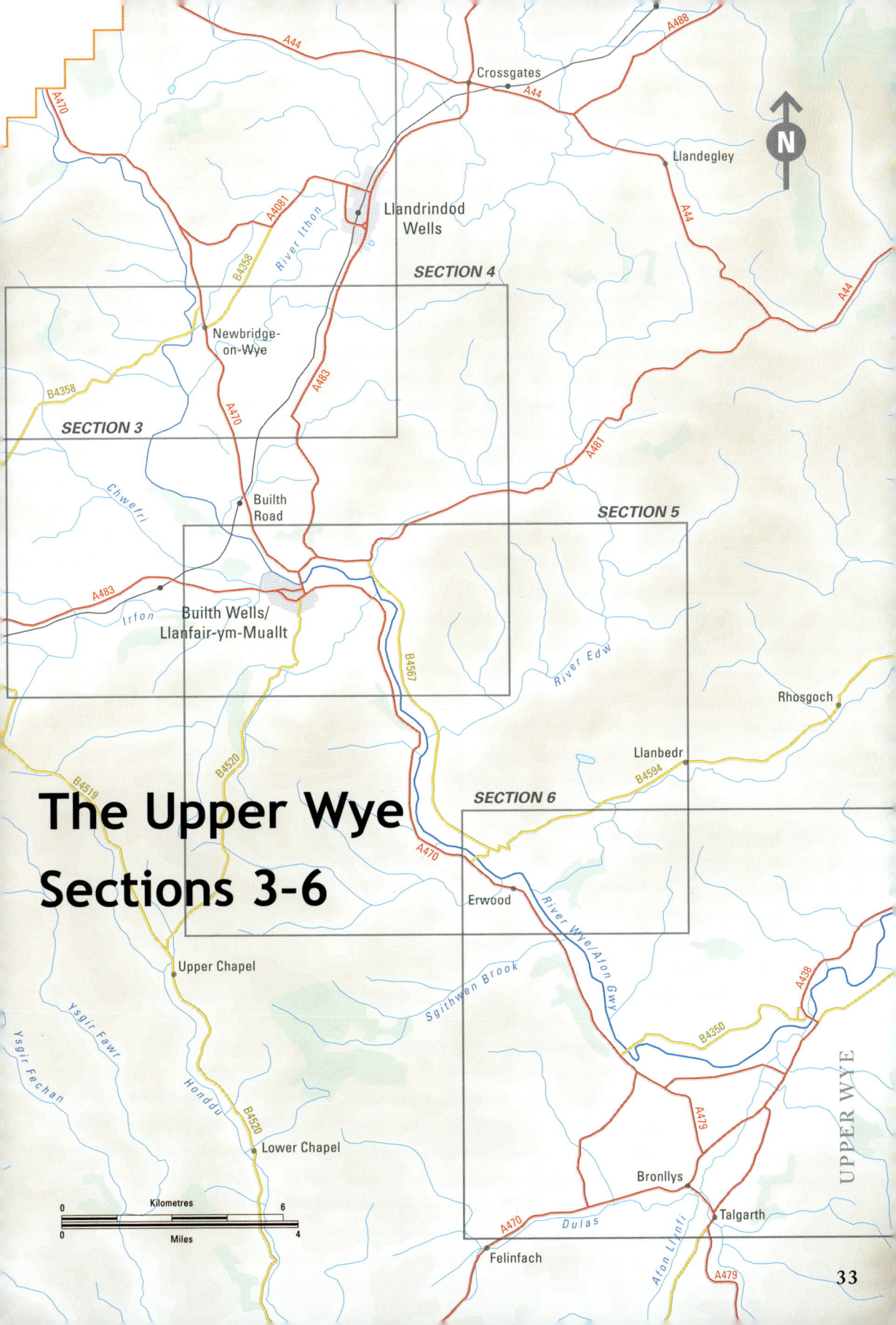

Headwaters of the River Wye.

Plynlimon summit.

Source of the Wye

Plynlimon

Distance	12km walk, following 7.2km of the Wye
Start	Source of the Wye SN 802 872
Finish	Pont Rhydgaled SN 841 827 / SY18 6SY
Difficulty	A tough boggy walk!

Introduction
The source of the Wye is located high on Plynlimon, a vast boggy mountain which also gives birth to the Severn and Rheidol rivers. Exploring the Wye's headwaters makes for a fine hill walk, revealing the river's truly wild origins.

Waypoints
Car park for Plynlimon walk SN 798 841 / SY23 3LE – there is a (charged) parking area in front of Eisteddfa Gurig farm.
Summit of Plynlimon SN 790 869
Source of the Wye SN 802 872
Pont Rhydgaled SN 841 827 / SY18 6SY – there is a Natural Resources Wales parking area on river right just below the bridge.

Description
The walk suggested here is to climb to the summit of Plynlimon by the normal footpath, and then perhaps to descend by following the Wye from its source down to the road at Pont Rhydgaled. Be equipped for mountain weather. The descent is away from waymarked routes; take a map and compass.

Park at Eisteddfa Gurig farm, beside the A44 Aberystwyth to Llangurig road. The farm's name translates as 'the seating place of St Curig'; the saint supposedly rested here, looked down into the Wye valley and decided to build a church at Llangurig.

The walk uphill is relatively straightforward; you are already over 400m above sea level, leaving only 350m to ascend! A track leads from the back of the farm beside the Afon Tarennig stream. After a couple of kilometres and just before some mining ruins, a small sign directs you away from the track to the left. It is now a steep climb up a winding and indistinct footpath 1.5km to the summit, where you cross a high stone wall to reach several large cairns, one of which doubles as a windbreak. Standing at the summit's triangulation point, you are 752m (2,468ft) above sea level, the highest point in Mid Wales. If the summit is clear of cloud (it generally isn't) the view extends north to the peaks of Snowdonia, west to the Cambrian Mountains, and south to the Brecon Beacons. This is a fine spot to reach,

📷 *Source of the River Wye.*

but for Wye aficionados, it's just your starting point. Just over a kilometre to the east is *Blaen Afon Gwy*, the source of the River Wye. You can take a bearing directly east from Plynlimon's summit, or follow the wall which runs atop the ridge. Either route brings you to a north-south aligned fence which sits atop the county boundary between Ceredigion and Powys. On the far side of the fence, a valley falls steeply away to the east; this is the Wye. Were you to follow this ridgetop about 3km NNE, you would reach the source of the Afon Hafren; the River Severn. The Wye and Severn originate side by side on Plynlimon, and meet again 120km to the SSE when the Wye disgorges into the Severn Estuary near Chepstow. Legend has it that the Wye, Severn and Rheidol challenged one another to a race, to see which river could reach the sea from Plynlimon first. The Rheidol won and the Severn is of course Britain's longest river, making the Wye something of a middle achiever.

Below the fence, three gullies emerge from the steep slope, about 100m apart. The Ordnance

📷 *Searching for the source.*

Survey designates the most northerly gully as the true source, but judge for yourself. If you descend to look closer, take care on this steep ground, especially in wet conditions. Robert Gibbings described the spot where the Wye commences as, *"a pool no bigger than a bowler hat"* (*Coming down the Wye* 1942). Water seeps out from bog moss, cottongrass and heather and trickles down to the 630m contour, where the three gullies converge. This spot is just 20km from the Irish Sea, but the Wye winds and loops for about 228km before reaching sea level at Bigsweir Bridge. You now have the option of backtracking to Plynlimon's summit and then retracing your route downhill to Eisteddfa Gurig farm.

A tougher but rewarding alternative is to follow the infant Wye downstream. The land is designated as Open Access under the CRoW Act, however choose your route carefully, both to minimise your impact on the environment and to avoid overly steep or boggy and tussocky ground. You will have to jump or wade across the Wye from time to time, so this is not an advisable undertaking when rain or snowmelt swells the flow.

Samuel Ireland was one of the few 18th century Wye Tour participants to venture to the source. Shortly after the source he encountered, *"an immense cataract, rolling with astonishing rapidity over the rocky prominences which seem to impede its course"* (*Picturesque Views on the River Wye* 1797). He didn't exaggerate. The river cuts down into the Ordovician geology in a series of steep flumes and waterfalls, falling over 100m. Pick

 *Headwaters.*

Flow gauge.

your way down slowly, and again in the following 1.5km which descends another 150m. Hidden in the bracken are mining remains such as tunnel entrances, former dams and (be careful!) open shafts.

A track head is reached on river left, making the going much easier. You will see flumes and rain gauges in this and adjoining streams, monitoring flows for the Centre for Ecology and Hydrology. The junction of the Wye and Nant y Gwrdy stream was the site of the Wye Valley Lead Mine from 1846–80, extracting lead and copper. The last mine in the valley closed in 1917. The buildings now present are home to the Sweet Lamb Rally Complex, a huge network of racing tracks.

The remaining 3km walk down the valley is simple, following the level track to the A44 at Pont Rhydgaled. Paddlers will of course find themselves mentally scoping out the river; this would be a practical paddling proposition in spate, but requires a walk-in carrying boats, as the estate office at Pont Rhydgaled have not previously proved keen to give permission to cars with boats on top. Below the rally buildings, it ambles at grade 2 and 3 with several sheep fences and a low pipe to negotiate. A tiny weir with three chutes is the only thing of note before a rocky fall at Llidiart Coch (grade 4?) which leads into a secluded grade 2 and 3 gorge, emerging at the A44 bridge.

Emerging at Pont Rhydgaled after this adventurous walk, your start point is 5km uphill along a fast and dangerous road; hopefully you shuttled a car here beforehand, as the walk back isn't to be recommended*.

*Actual author experience.

Fall downstream of Pont Rhydgaled

Llangurig church.

Section 1

Pont Rhydgaled to Pont Llangurig

Distance	9.8km
Start	Pont Rhydgaled SN 841 827 / SY18 6SY
Finish	Pont Llangurig SN 908 797 / SY18 6SG
Difficulty	Grade 4 at first, easing to grade 2

Introduction
Very few paddlers venture this far up the Wye … which is surprising, because the river provides some real excitement while carving its route from Plynlimon down into an open plain.

Launch points
Pont Rhydgaled SN 841 827 / SY18 6SY – there is a Natural Resources Wales parking area on river right just below the bridge. Launch wherever suits.

Pont Llangurig SN 908 797 / SY18 6SG – limited roadside parking. Access river left, downstream of bridge.

Nearby attractions
Plynlimon is no doubt the main attraction hereabouts! West along the A44 are the spectacular waterfalls at Devil's Bridge, the Silver Mining Museum at Llywernog and Nant yr Arian Forest, which has mountain bike trails and also red kite feeding.

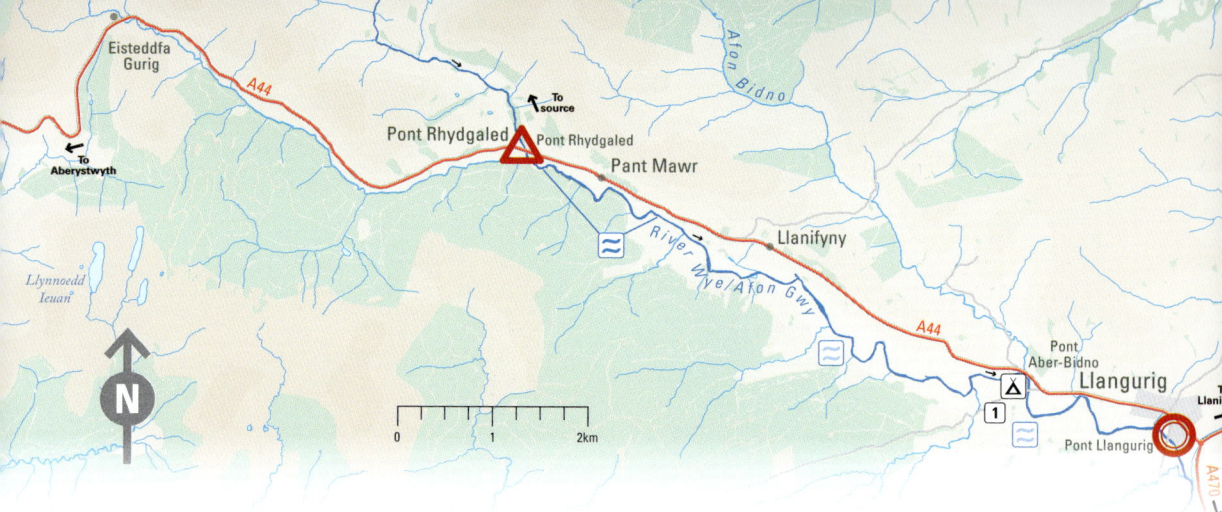

Accommodation

There is one campsite in this valley, the very pleasant Glangwy Farm Camping. B&B and hotel information is available from the Tourist Information Centre in Aberystwyth 01970 612125.

Description

For a good paddle, it needs to have rained heavily in the previous 24 hours. At the put-in, the entire riverbed needs to be well covered. Exercise caution in full spate as the falls near the start will produce some munchy stoppers, and the low-hanging wire strands near the end will be dangerous.

The Wye meets the A44 at Pont Rhydgaled on the Aberystwyth to Llangurig road. This bleak spot didn't have a passable road until 1830, when a direct coach route was opened up from the Midlands to the Mid Wales coast. At this point the Wye has flowed only 7.2km from its source, but has been joined by many tributaries swelling its size. The last of these is the Afon Tarennig which merges from river right at the put-in; henceforth the Wye is no longer a moorland ditch. Incidentally, the Tarennig has plenty of steep whitewater if you want to extend your adventure.

There isn't any warm-up. Almost around the first corner, the first of perhaps four distinct back-to-back grade 4 rapids is encountered. Inspect on river left as the river right bank is hemmed in by coniferous forest. Over several hundred metres, the Wye thunders over a series of ledges and rocky reefs; a weir is marked on the 1:25,000 Ordnance Survey map, but all of these river features are formed by natural bedrock. At low paddleable levels there isn't too much which can go wrong here, but in high flows powerful stoppers form, the rapids merge and it all becomes rather consequential. Note that no published whitewater guidebook mentions these rapids (which can be glimpsed from the main road!), and some describe the Wye above Llangurig as grade 2. If you just came for the short but sweet section of technical whitewater, one possibility is to walk out to the road along a footpath, maybe that at Llanifyny. However paddling

Ledge drops.

on to Llangurig is not a hardship; the river is always fast-flowing and the distance passes away quickly. Indeed, you might well want to keep on going past Llangurig, where the whitewater cranks up once again.

The valley opens out after the last fall and the Wye meanders through farmland. From the road, this all looks flat, but there are frequent grade 2 rapids where the river narrows and steepens. The scenery is rather grand, with mountains forming the backdrop on all sides and the dense conifers replaced by oak, ash, alder and willow trees. In spring, woodland birds such as redstarts and tree pipits venture this far up the valley, making it easy to forget that you are 300m above sea level.

The Afon Bidno joins from river left beneath Pont Aber-Bidno, and then the Wye passes under a road bridge which shouldn't be mistaken for the take-out bridge 2km further on. This final stretch sees the river become much wider. Be careful; the pebble banks and shoals on the riverbed are spawning grounds for salmon which have completed the journey upriver. Unfortunately there are several wire and rope strands stretched across the river as you approach Llangurig; all are straightforward to duck in low or medium levels, but stay alert for this wholly unnecessary artificial hazard.

The sight of a church spire marks your imminent arrival at the village of Llangurig, and soon Pont Llangurig is reached. Perched at 288m above sea level, Llangurig dubiously claims to be Wales's highest village. It takes its name from St Curig who founded a monastery here in the 6th century; the current church is dedicated to St Curig and dates from the 15th century, but was restored in 1878.

At this point, the River Severn – which emerged on Plynlimon – is only 5km away, to the north. However, the Wye now swings south and flows towards a cleft in the hills.

Rhayader Town Falls.

Rhayader Town Falls.

Section 2

Pont Llangurig to Rhayader

Distance	16.4km
Start	Pont Llangurig SN 908 797 / SY18 6SG
Finish	Rhayader SN 969 677 / LD6 5AL
Difficulty	Grade 3 rapids with one grade 4 waterfall

Introduction

The Wye narrows through a cleft in the Cambrian Mountains, flowing over or squeezing through whorled bedrock to produce the most sustained section of rapids on the whole river. A classic whitewater trip, to be tackled by those with advanced whitewater skills and using specialist craft; this is no place for touring canoes!

Launch points

Pont Llangurig SN 908 797 / SY18 6SG – limited roadside parking. Access the water downstream side of the bridge on river left.

Dolhelfa SN 921 738 / SY18 6RY – a small turn off the A470 is signposted 'Dernol'; this leads down to the river. On the river right downstream side of the bridge, pass through two gates to reach the water.

Pont Marteg SN 951 716 / LD6 5LE – a ramp leads down to the river from the large lay-by and parking area just north of Pont Marteg. River left.

Rhayader SN 969 677 / LD6 5AL – park beside the rugby club. A rough track leads to the water on river left, 100m downstream of the Town Falls.

Above Pont Marteg.

Nearby attractions

There is good walking and mountain-biking around Llangurig, especially to the south-west. A visit to Gilfach Nature Reserve, a stunning 162ha SSSI, is recommended.

Accommodation

Wyeside Camping and Caravanning Club Site is located beside the river in Rhayader. Mid Wales Bunkhouse, Tipi and Camping and Beili Neuadd Bunkhouse are located nearby. B&B and hotel information can be obtained from the Tourist Information Centre in Llandrindod Wells 01597 822600.

Description

This trip is at its best after significant recent rain. Judge the level by looking at Town Falls, beneath the bridge in Rhayader. If there is no central rocky island between the fish pass on river left and the fall on river right, the river is high; an ideal medium level would be for this island to be showing but for the fall on river right to be well covered. This trip is not pleasant in very low paddleable levels as the bedrock channels paddlers into claustrophobic and uninviting constrictions.

The first half of this trip is easier and often missed out by launching at Dolhelfa, but with at least a medium flow, it's all good; launch at Llangurig. The flow from the start is swift, but overgrown bushes and trees loom overhead and trail in the water, forming a somewhat gloomy tunnel. Thankfully the banks soon open out and the stunning mountain backdrop can be enjoyed. The whitewater interest builds with a series of three small natural weirs, perhaps grade 3. The following two rapids are most definitely grade 3; the first being an exhilarating flume jetting forcefully into a sharp left bend, and the second being a sharp drop in height on a left bend. After this, bouncy waves lead down to the bridge near Dolhelfa.

From Dolhelfa's bridge, you will spy the towering sails of Bryn Titli Wind Farm atop the mountain on river left; built in 1994, this was the first in Wales. While gazing uphill, keep an eye out for the soaring buzzard, peregrine falcon and red kite whose domain this really is.

The valley sides soon close in further and the first indication of a change in the river's character comes when the water accelerates towards a large boulder perched in mid-flow … what to do? You've reached the start of what Thomas Roscoe described as, *"one continued series of rapids and cascades"* (*Wanderings and Excursions in South Wales* 1837) where the Wye flows over, through and around whorled bedrock. There are at least five distinct and technical grade 3 rapids to negotiate before the confluence of the Afon Marteg, and a further four before Rhayader, although in high water they merge and become a fluffier and less technical proposition. Roscoe also noted, *"Very, very beautiful is that wood-hung, torrent-ravine"*, and indeed the paddler should find time to appreciate the dripping ferns hanging along the banks, and the dippers which flit from rock to rock looking for insects. If the water is not too murky, you may spy salmon, trout and even brook lamprey lurking in the shadows of deep pools. You are passing through the heart of Radnorshire Wildlife Trust's 'Cwm Marteg Living Landscape' and it's all rather nice.

A track leading up to the A470 on river left

 *Below Pont Marteg.*

Wye valley near Pont Marteg.

is a possible evacuation point, just before the Marteg flows beneath Pont Marteg out of Gilfach Nature Reserve on river left. The way ahead seems barred by the mountain of Gamallt, but the Wye bends sharp right and the valley sides open out just enough for the rapids to become more spaced apart. Beside one steep fall by a disused railway bridge, look back upstream to see a metal 'human' sculpture hanging from a bridge pillar.

When caravans are seen on river left (Wyeside Camping and Caravanning Club Site), you are entering Rhayader. Several fast-flowing channelled rapids keep the adrenaline flowing; one was previously the site of 'Castle Weir', named for Rhayader Castle which was sited on Castle Hill to the left. The river pools before the B4518 bridge, a place to regroup as Town Falls is directly downstream. With care, it's possible to paddle through the stopper beneath the bridge and then eddy out on the left to inspect or portage. Although the Town Falls (grade 4) were blasted in the 1780s to reduce the size of the fall, and have had fish steps added (don't paddle these), Roscoe's 1837 description still suits: *"The Wye ... rushes through the one grand and lofty arch of the bridge, and flowing rapidly onwards, is suddenly flung over a group of rugged masses of rock, forming a wide, varied and beautiful cascade."*

If you find yourself inspecting or providing safety cover, take a few moments to study the innumerable elaborate whorls in the rock, large and small, and ponder the passage of time.

The take-out is directly below on river left, where a byway leads away from the river. It's a short walk up to the rugby club car park.

Below Llanwrthwl.

Above Llanwrthwl.

Section 3

Rhayader to Newbridge-on-Wye

Distance	14.7km
Start	Rhayader SN 969 677 / LD6 5AL
Finish	Newbridge SO 014 583 / LD1 6LY
Difficulty	Grade 2 rapids with one grade 3

Introduction

This section sees the Wye's last exertions as a mountain stream, before it is joined by the Afon Elan and significantly expands in width and volume. The rapids keep coming and this is an excellent introduction to technical whitewater.

Launch points

Rhayader SN 969 677 / LD6 5AL – park beside the rugby club. A rough track leads to the water on river left, 100m downstream of Rhayader Bridge.

Llanwrthwl Bridge SN 976 640 / LD1 6NS – limited roadside parking near the bridge. Pass through the gate on the downstream side, river left.

Wye Bridge, at Newbridge SO 014 583 / LD1 6LY – on river right of the bridge there is a lay-by for parking. A football club parking area across the road can be used for loading; a path leads to the river upstream of the bridge.

Nearby attractions

Gigrin Farm Red Kite Centre is the place to see these birds up close. The Elan Valley dams are an unmissable landscape, with a visitor centre and cycle trails.

Accommodation

Wyeside Camping and Caravanning Club Site is located beside the river in Rhayader. Doliago Farm campsite is near Llanwrthwl. Oak Grove Retreats at Doldowlod Caravan Park is beside the river and has a few camping pitches. B&B

and hotel information can be obtained from the tourist information centre in Llandrindod Wells on 01597 822600.

Description

The market town of Rhayader takes its name from the Welsh *Rhaeadr Gwy* – 'Fall of the Wye'. This trip begins just below these falls, launching from a byway on river left, opposite a park and children's play area. Recent rain is ideal to cover over the rockier sections downstream, although high water needs treating with respect as it can be tricky to get a swimmer out. Passing St Bride's Church on river right, the river bends left and flows towards the A470 before turning right again. If your paddle coincides with feeding time at Gigrin Farm, the sky will be thick with hundreds of wheeling red kites ... quite a spectacle. As you leave Rhayader, a series of small ledges form a grade 2+ rapid beneath a pipe bridge. Large boulders in the river form further grade 2 rapids in the following kilometres, a good warm-up for where the river funnels towards a disused railway bridge; hop out and inspect on the right! A long grade 3 rapid bounces paddlers down to the Afon Elan which joins from river right.

The Elan is among the Wye's largest tributaries, but the flow is controlled by a series of massive dams constructed along the valley from the 1890s, to create a water supply for Birmingham. The confluence is a striking spot with wide vistas, as noted by Louisa Anne

Inspecting the railway bridge rapid.

Rainy paddle below Llanwrthwl.

Craig Coch dam.

Doldowlod House.

Twamley who ventured here from her native Midlands, *"the vales of both rivers are in view for some distance"* (*An Autumn Ramble by the Wye* 1839). The hillside to river right is the vast RSPB Carngaffallt reserve, where red kite, buzzard, stonechat and redstart are protected. Shortly downstream, a rocky natural weir leads into a series of gravel braids above a footbridge. The kilometre down to Llanwrthwl Bridge is continuous grade 2+, which will test boulder dodging skills in lower levels, and swamp a few canoes in high water. The final exertions of these rapids lead around an island to the concrete Llanwrthwl Bridge, where some might wish to end (or start) the trip, the whitewater downstream being much milder.

Below Llanwrthwl, the river's pace slackens, but there are many grade 2 wave trains, decreasing in frequency towards Newbridge.

The Wye winds beneath the bracken-covered sides of two mountains which successively dominate the view ahead; the 475m high Trembyd, the eastern edge of one of the largest areas of common land in Wales, then the 442m Rhiw Gwraidd. The grounds of Doldowlod House are then passed on river left. This impressive gothic mansion was bought by steam engine pioneer James Watt and 'improved' around 1827 by his son James Watt Jr. who erected three suspension bridges to connect his estate across the river. The Watts' descendants still own the estate but only one of the bridges remains, at Ystrad. Paddlers will spot the quirky and somewhat incongruous statue of a Hindu deity overlooking the river from the grounds of the house.

The imminence of journey's end at Newbridge is indicated when Llysdinam Hall is seen on the hillside ahead. The river bends sharply left in front of this, flowing over pebbly reefs around a solitary beleaguered tree – how long will this survive? Wye Bridge is a grim concrete slab, egress on river right just below.

The Rebecca Riots

Rhayader was central to the bizarre 'Rebecca Riots' which erupted across Wales in 1843–44. Resenting heavy tolls charged to use turnpikes (roads), armed men disguised by blackened faces and women's clothing would venture forth by night to break the hated tollgates. They called themselves 'Rebecca and her daughters', inspired by the biblical Rebecca of whom the *Book of Genesis* says, *"Let thy seed possess the gates of those who hate them"*. Six Rhayader tollgates were destroyed, the one at Cwmdauddwr being dumped into the Wye. The Metropolitan Police were called in from London to restore order! Tempers eased after Parliament reduced tolls with the 1844 Turnpike Act. However, Rebecca and her rebellious daughters popped up locally for decades after, using the guise to illegally spear salmon by torchlight.

Penygarreg Reservoir.

Surfing below Llanwrthwl.

Just below Newbridge.

Penddol Rocks. Photo | Eurion Brown.

Section 4

Newbridge-on-Wye to Builth Wells

Distance	11.3km
Start	Newbridge SO 014 583 / LD1 6LY
Finish	Builth Wells SO 042 511 / LD2 3DW
Difficulty	Grade 2 rapids with one grade 3

Introduction
This section of the Wye flows quietly away from civilisation, gradually expanding into a major river as tributaries join. Those looking for whitewater may find things slow to start with, but the trip builds to a dramatic and surprising conclusion.

Launch points
Wye Bridge, at Newbridge SO 014 583 / LD1 6LY – on river right of the bridge there is a lay-by for parking. A football club parking area across the road can be used for loading; a path leads to the river upstream of the bridge. Builth Wells SO 042 511 / LD2 3DW – The Groe car park is on river right above Wye Bridge. Launch near the bull statue.

Nearby attractions
Little is happening here ...

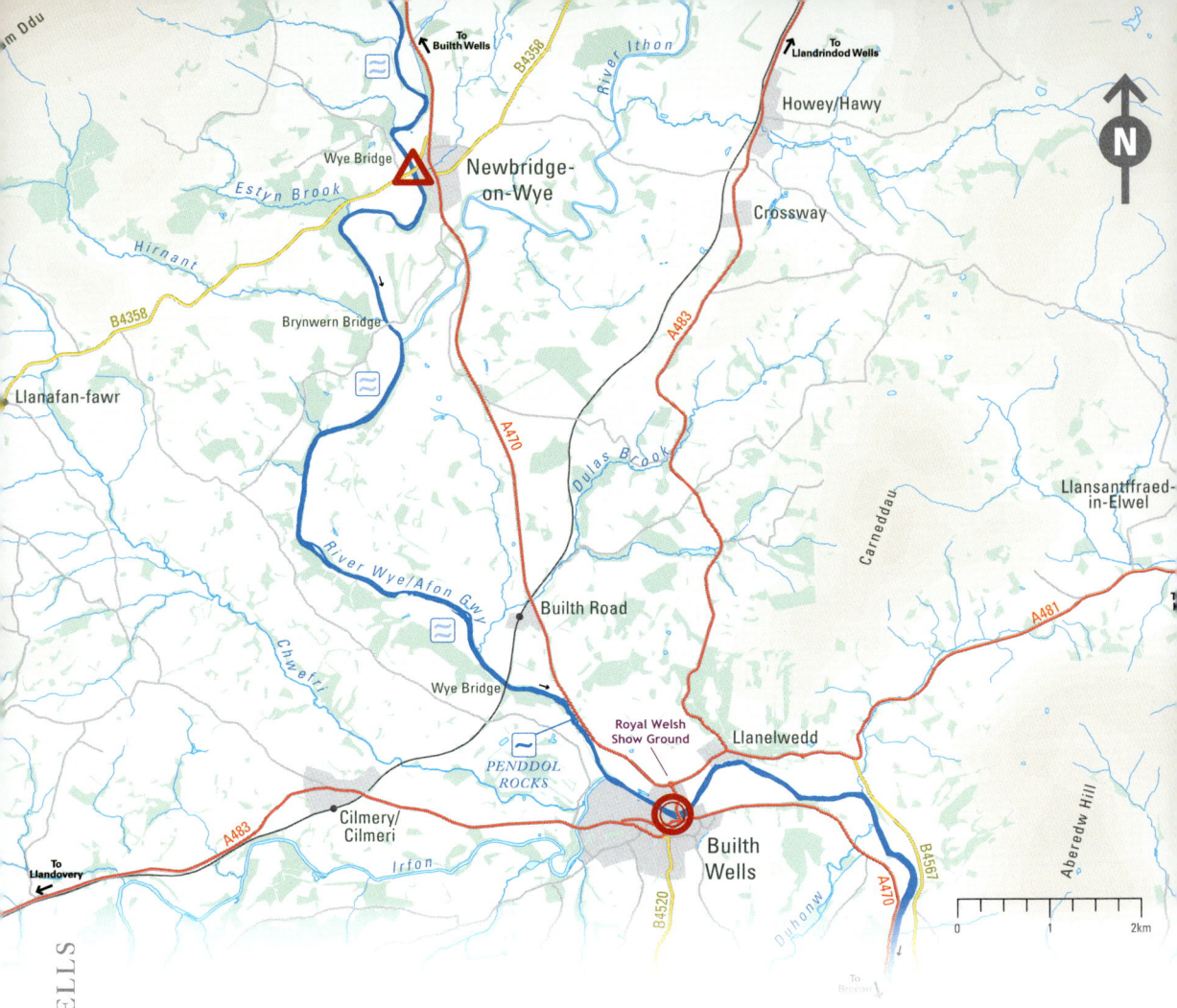

Accommodation

There are no campsites along the river on this section. B&B and hotel information can be obtained from the tourist information centre in Llandrindod Wells on 01597 822600.

Description

"Grand scenery; lofty banks; woody vales; a rocky channel, and a rapid stream" (Thomas Dudley Fosbroke, *The Wye Tour* 1822)

Newbridge-on-Wye's bridge is called Wye Bridge and isn't especially new, dating from 1981. The town's name however originates from the first of successive bridges dating back around two centuries, before which this was the site of an ancient drover's ford.

The Wye is by now a full-sized river. The backdrop is still mountainous, but the surrounding farmland is lowland, with more cows than sheep! The flora and fauna are also less upland in character, with oak, ash and alder trees along the banks, wildflowers proliferating from Newbridge downstream, and pied flycatchers and willow warblers being seen in spring and early summer. Fishermen note this as the point where coarse fishing begins, and fewer trout are caught.

There are few rapids in the 3km down to Brynwern Bridge. A number of pools or *llyns* are marked on the 1:25,000 Ordnance Survey map; these are important fishing spots. Brynwern Bridge is an unprepossessing modern affair, but the grounds of Bryn-wern Hall below on river right are more interesting; this large house was designed by Stephen Williams, who built Erwood Bridge (section 5). Also just below the bridge is the confluence of the River Ithon from river left, which emerges flowing rapidly beneath a sandstone cliff. This has a huge catchment and often carries more water than the Wye. The Ithon seems to revive the Wye, as henceforth there are frequent grade 2 rapids. These sometimes braid around banks and islands, giving a choice of route.

The railway bridge encountered after 9km is another Wye Bridge (there will be many more). Unlike most railway bridges along the Wye, this is still in use, carrying the 'Heart of Wales' line which connects Shrewsbury and South Wales. This bridge is of most interest to paddlers as a warning of the approach of Penddol Rocks. A few hundred metres past the bridge, a series of bedrock reefs spanning the river precipitate a complete change in its character. Hop ashore and inspect this long and complex grade 3 rapid from river right. A choice of rocky channels descend past an island, with limited opportunity to stop before

Penddol Rocks – the determined approach!.

the whole river is contorted through a boily S-bend. At lower water levels, this will test your manoeuvring skills, especially in an open canoe! In high water, the water backs up at the constriction, forming an unpredictable and surging sudden drop in height into the pool below. The rapid eases off through a final cluster of rocks, some of which are connected by fishing jetties (called 'croys').

Penddol Rocks seem to expend all of the river's energy, as the final kilometre into Builth Wells is flat. The Afon Irfon joins on river right, marking the start of The Groe. Historically, this open space along the river right bank was where the folk of Builth met and grazed their animals. In the 19th century it became a leisure park, with a weir forming a boating pool, which was eventually swept away by floods. Take out onto The Groe just before Wye Bridge, close to the bull statue.

Wye Bridge, Builth Wells

Above Erwood Bridge.

Section 5

Builth Wells to Erwood

Distance	13.8km
Start	Builth Wells SO 042 511 / LD2 3DW
Finish	Erwood SO 105 428 / LD2 3SZ
Difficulty	Grade 1 and 2 rapids

Introduction

Below Builth Wells, the mountains close in once more, and many rate this as the most scenic part of the entire river. The rapids are intermittent, with the longest conveniently towards the end. They are also easy, with none of the 'extreme' stuff found on the sections above and below.

Launch points

Builth Wells SO 042 511 / LD2 3DW – The Groe car park is on river right above Wye Bridge. Launch near the bull statue.

Erwood SO 105 428 / LD2 3SZ – from the A470, cross Erwood Bridge and turn right. After about 2km, park in a lay-by just before the bridge across the Nant Bachawy stream. Park, cross the bridge and take the footpath down to the Wye.

Nearby attractions

A walk up around Aberedw Rocks offers great views of the river. Wyeside Arts Centre is close to Wye Bridge in Builth Wells. At Llanelwedd, opposite on the river left bank, is the

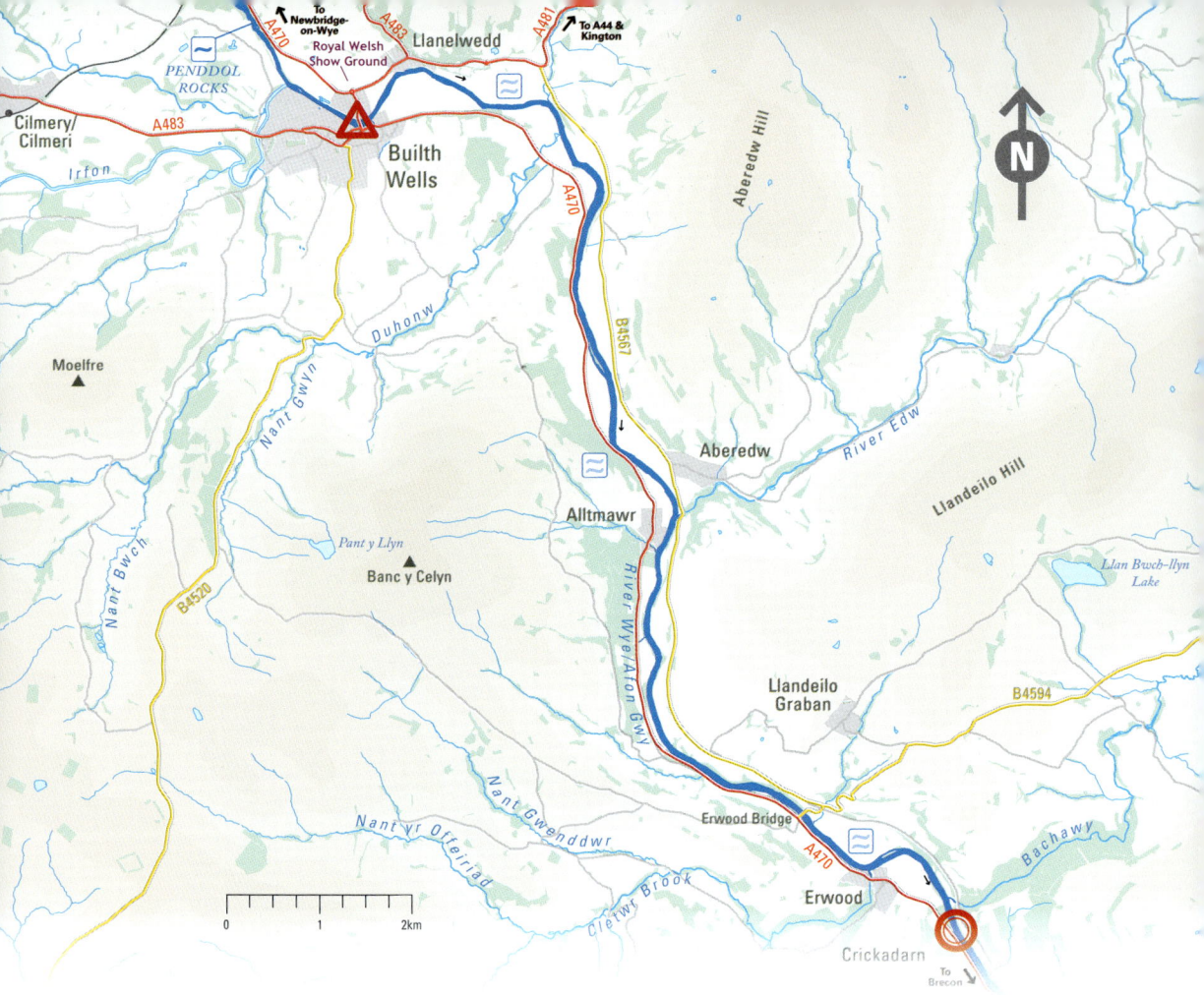

Royal Welsh Showground; this hosts the Royal Welsh Show (the biggest agricultural show in Europe) for four days every July, and the Royal Welsh Agricultural Winter Fair in December.

Accommodation

There are no campsites along the river on this section. B&B and hotel information can be obtained from the tourist information centre in Llandrindod Wells on 01597 822600.

Description

"Huge mountains on either side confine the valley as we advance. Aberedw Hill rises on the left bank; and Allt Mawr, on the right, erects its stern precipitous front huge and frowningly". (Thomas Roscoe, *Scenery of the River Wye* c. 1839)

Builth Wells' name has both Welsh and English components. The Welsh *Buallt* comes from *bu* (ox) and *allt* (wooded height), while Wells is a reference to the mineral springs at nearby Park Wells and Glanne Wells. To complicate

📷 *Above Erwood Bridge.*

things further, the full Welsh name is *Llanfair-ym-Muallt* – Church of Our Lady in Buallt. Wye Bridge has been in place since it was built in 1779, but did however require reconstruction after the great flood of 1795. Directly below the bridge on river right is the motte (earth mound) of Builth Castle. Little is left of the castle as the stone was used to rebuild the town following a fire in 1690. A rapid leads paddlers from the bridge straight towards Llanelwedd Quarries, a vast gaping scar in the mountain of Carneddau. The Wye bends away to the right as it gradually turns south, and thankfully the environment is henceforth always attractive and unspoiled.

The small Blaen Duhonw stream joins from river right, heralding a narrowing of the valley, such that the hills almost rise direct from the river. The Cambrian Railway Line is squeezed along the river left bank throughout this trip. It was opened in 1864 but is now sadly disused, having been a victim of the Beeching Report in the early 1960s. Rapids at this point are mild and intermittent, little more than choppy waves kicked up by funnelling gravel banks.

The Afon Edw which joins from river left is famous for trout and eels; this river is overshadowed by the impressive Aberedw Rocks, a series of crags which tower 200m above the Wye. Up among these crags is Llewelyn's Cave, reputedly the final hiding place of the last Welsh Prince.

The last Prince of Wales

Builth Castle was rebuilt in stone from 1277–82 by the English King Edward I, notorious for his fierce subjugation of the Welsh nation (and similarly, as the 'Hammer of the Scots'). Edward faced repeated resistance from Llewellyn ap Gruffydd, the last native Prince of Wales. In December 1282, Llewellyn sought refuge in the castle, but was refused entry; for long after, the townsfolk were labelled *Bradwyr Buallt* (the traitors of Builth). Llewellyn was forced to turn and face the English army. The Battle of Irfon Bridge, just west of Builth, saw the Welsh army totally routed. Some accounts claim that Llewellyn was killed in battle by a spear, others that he fled south to Aberedw, high above the Wye. In this version, he asked local blacksmith Madoc Coch to aid him in escaping through the snow by reversing his horse's shoes, to confuse the pursuing English. The blacksmith betrayed Llewellyn to the English and the hapless prince was hunted down and beheaded at the cave where he was hiding. The last Prince of Wales is commemorated by a 1956 monolith at Cilmery (site of the battle) and by a prominent mural in Builth.

The Builth Wells Bull.

Approaching Erwood Bridge, the rapids become longer and the waves larger, channelled by angled bedrock. In full spate, these slabs generate waves large and steep enough to attract expert playboaters. Erwood Station is located on river left just upstream of the bridge; this has reopened as an art gallery and tea room. Incidentally, the name Erwood means ford – *y rhyd*. This was indeed once a crossing for cattle drovers. The modern bridge replaced a Victorian lattice-girdered toll bridge.

Your takeout is just after the tiny Bachawy stream enters on river left. If the rapids around Erwood Bridge have left you unsatiated, consider continuing into section 6, as far as Boughrood Bridge.

Glasbury launching ban

Early in 2021, Powys Council 'temporarily' banned launching from Glasbury Common. They did not ban any of the other activities which take place here (picnicking, dog-walking, wild swimming and so forth) and these continue unrestricted. The reason given was that Natural Resources Wales required them to carry out a 'Habitat Regulations Assessment' of the impact of paddling on both the immediate locale and the River Wye Special Area of Conservation. Launching by canoe hire companies based elsewhere at Glasbury was not banned and continues as before.

By Autumn 2021, Powys Council had investigated funding possibilities for this project. At time of writing (January 2022), it seems unlikely that public access to launch on the River Wye at Glasbury will be restored any time soon. Additionally, it is clear that attempting to impose restrictions on paddlers accessing the river here is seriously being considered. For updates on this situation, check the Canoe Wales website. Until this is resolved, paddlers will have to launch either up- or downstream of Glasbury.

Approaching Hell Hole.

Hell Hole.

Section 6

Erwood to Glasbury

Distance 11.9km
Start Erwood SO 105 428 / LD2 3SZ
Finish Glasbury SO 179 392 / HR3 5NW
Difficulty Grade 1 and 2 with two grade 3 rapids

Introduction

This trip marks the transition from the Upper to the Middle Wye. Some exciting rapids are the final reminders of the Wye's upland heritage, before the river emerges from the Cambrian Mountains and the flow slows and braids out across a wide floodplain.

Launch points

Erwood SO 105 428 / LD2 3SZ – from the A470, cross Erwood Bridge and turn right. After about 2km, park in a lay-by just before the bridge across the Nant Bachawy stream. Park, cross the bridge and take the footpath down to the Wye.

Boughrood Bridge SO 130 384 / LD3 0YB – park in the primary school car park on river right. A path leads to the river, upstream of the bridge.

Glasbury Bridge SO 179 392 / HR3 5NW – park outside the scout hut, upstream of the bridge on river left. The river is reached through a gate. Launching or landing here was temporarily banned in 2021, see boxed text on page 65 for details.

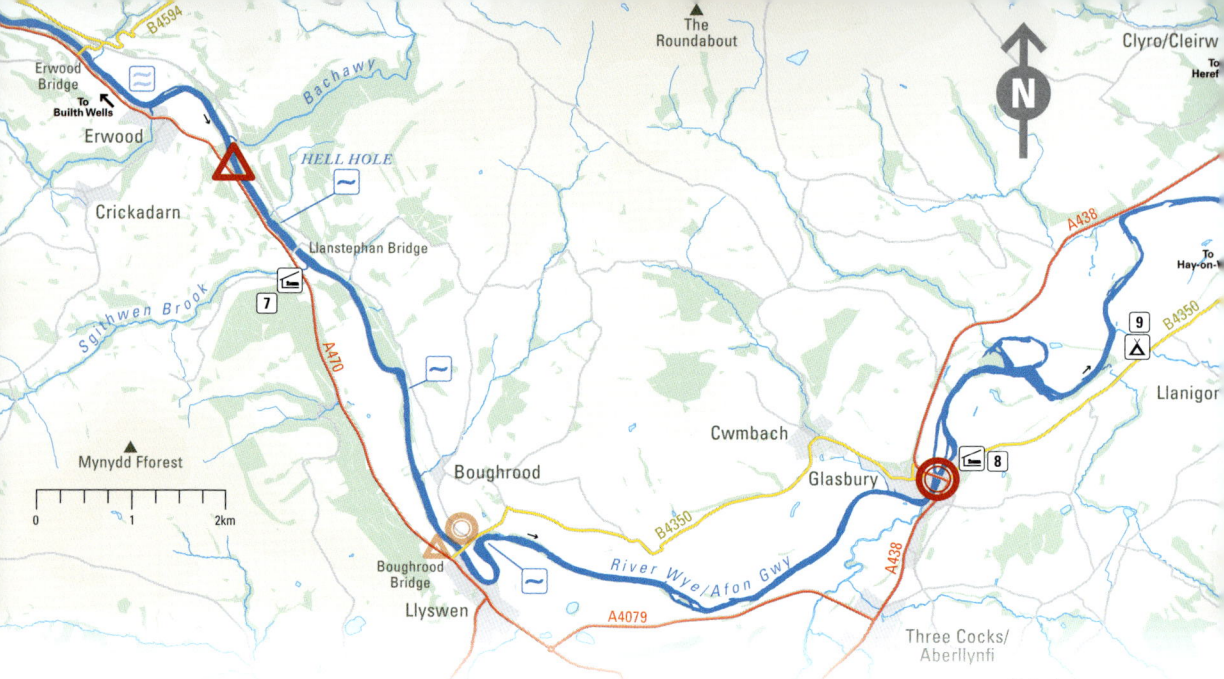

Nearby attractions

Talgarth is a few miles south on the edge of the Brecon Beacons National Park, and is a great base for outdoor activities. Bronllys Castle makes for a good dose of history.

Accommodation

River Cabin Camping is near to the river below Llanstephan Bridge. B&B and hotel information can be obtained from the tourist information centre in Llandrindod Wells on 01597 822600.

Description

Launching below the Nant Bachawy stream, take a moment to enjoy the wild chives which are common along the lime-rich riverside rocks here. There will be plenty more opportunity to soak up the surroundings, as this trip is predominantly flat water ... however, hold off on this when you launch, as the first and largest rapid is only 800m from the start!

Llanstephan Bridge is a wood-decked suspension bridge dating from 1922, the only such bridge in Wales and the only suspension bridge carrying vehicles on the Wye. It's unmistakeable and indeed you'll be keen not to mistake it as it is just downstream of 'Hell Hole'. Don't be put off by the name. Hop out to inspect from the rocky slab on river right and judge this grade 3 rapid for yourself. Several ledges in succession slant diagonally across the width of the river. At lower water levels, most of the flow gurgles down a narrow chute alongside the river right bank; paddlers will have to contend with avoiding the rocky wall, as well as surprisingly powerful boils and swirls. As the water level rises, a plethora of route options opens up, and the ledges begin to kick up sizeable waves and stoppers across the whole width – one of these must be the eponymous 'Hell Hole'! In spate, these features become truly huge and the rapid is probably grade 4.

Below Llanstephan Bridge, the Wye seems to have eased, with sporadic small rapids interspersed by long pools of calm. However, a sneaky ambush awaits around a right bend. With little warning, a steep tricky rapid pours over a sudden ledge. If you capsize and take an unplanned swim here, you won't be the first to have done so ('cough cough').

You are now passing Llangoed Hall, where sweet chestnut and oak trees planted 200 years ago can be seen along the banks. The 2km to Boughrood Bridge is largely flat, and those who just came for the excitement of Hell Hole may wish to egress here. The bridge's six arches link Boughrood (river left) with Llyswen (river right) and was opened in 1842 as a toll bridge; the toll house is still there on the Llyswen side. Boughrood's name comes from *bach-rhyd* (little ford) and the Boat Inn is a reminder that this was a ferry point before the bridge was built. 'Llyswen' means 'White Court' which is believed to refer to an Early Medieval law-making assembly, presided over by an early King of Wales, Rhodri Mawr (c. 820–878).

The Wye has one last dramatic flourish before leaving the mountains; it bends sharply back on itself, almost reaching Boughrood Bridge once more! As it flows past Boughrood itself, the Wye bends back on itself again, with a very long, stepped grade 2 rapid to enjoy.

This is the point where the Wye departs the underlying Mid Wales geology of grey shales to now flow through a landscape of Old Red Sandstone. The dark red soil which is revealed along the banks by water erosion was itself produced by erosion of the sandstone. Although the English border is still 12km east as the crow flies, this soil is a classic feature of Herefordshire's landscape and will characterise the Middle Wye right through to Ross-on-Wye. With more yielding banks and a wider plain, the Wye spreads out and occasionally braids around islands and shoals. The rapids are just grade 1, but the scenery keeps you engaged; now dramatically revealed along the south (river right) bank are the Black Mountains, a series of steep bluffs soaring 600m above the Wye.

As you enter the village of Glasbury, the Afon Llynfi joins from river right and the river widens above Glasbury Bridge. Take out upstream of this, on the left.

The Great Flood of 1795

Numerous floods have been historically recorded on the Wye, but that of 1795 stands out due to the devastation it wrought. A long and harsh winter in the Cambrian Mountains was followed by a rapid warming. The resulting flood surge destroyed every single bridge across the Wye in Wales. Samuel Ireland described the impact on Glasbury's seven-arched stone bridge: *"It is at present little more than a wreck; every arch of it having been blown up by the torrent of ice, which poured down on the very sudden thaw, after the long frost in the beginning of 1795"*. (*Picturesque Views on the River Wye* 1797)

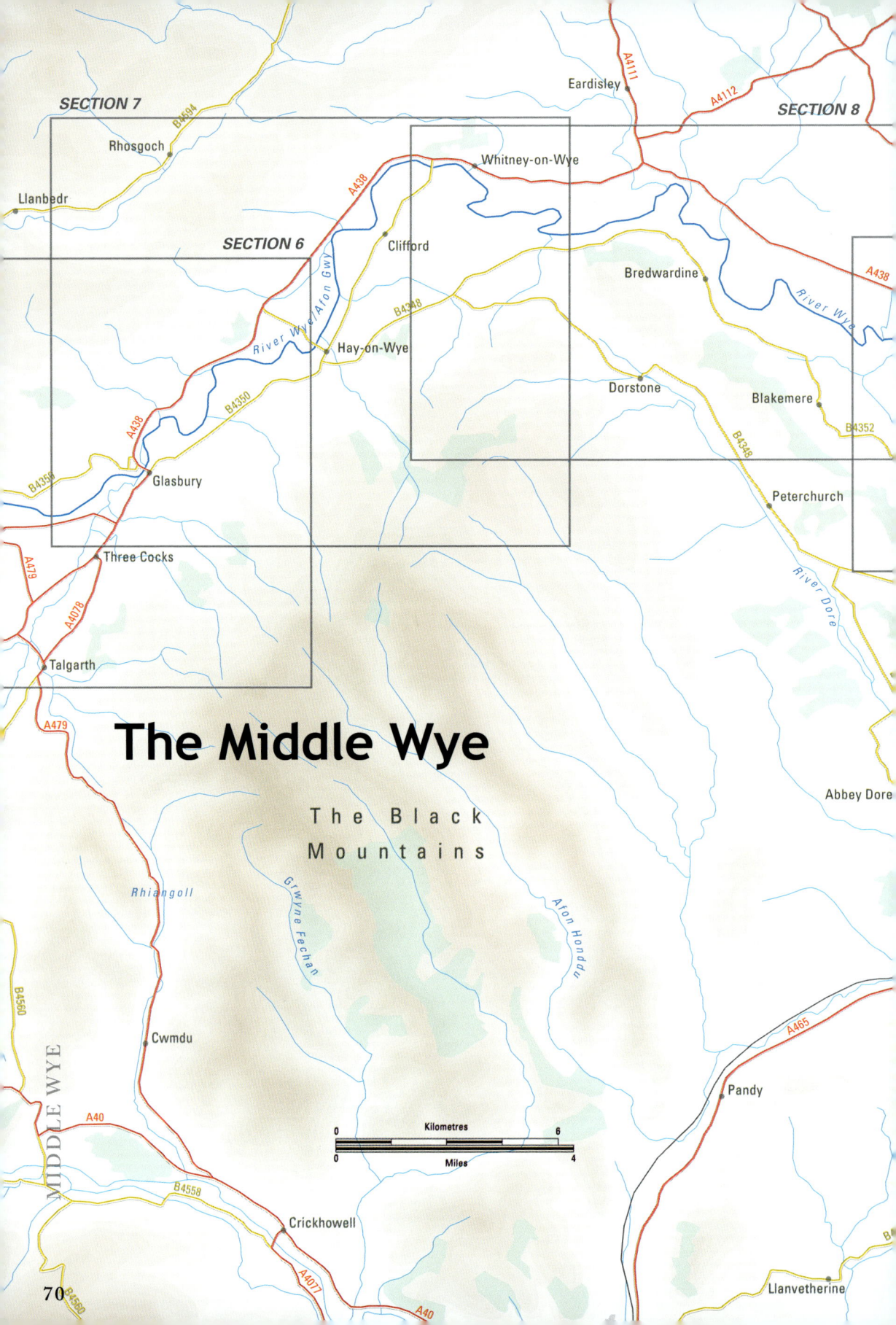

The Middle Wye

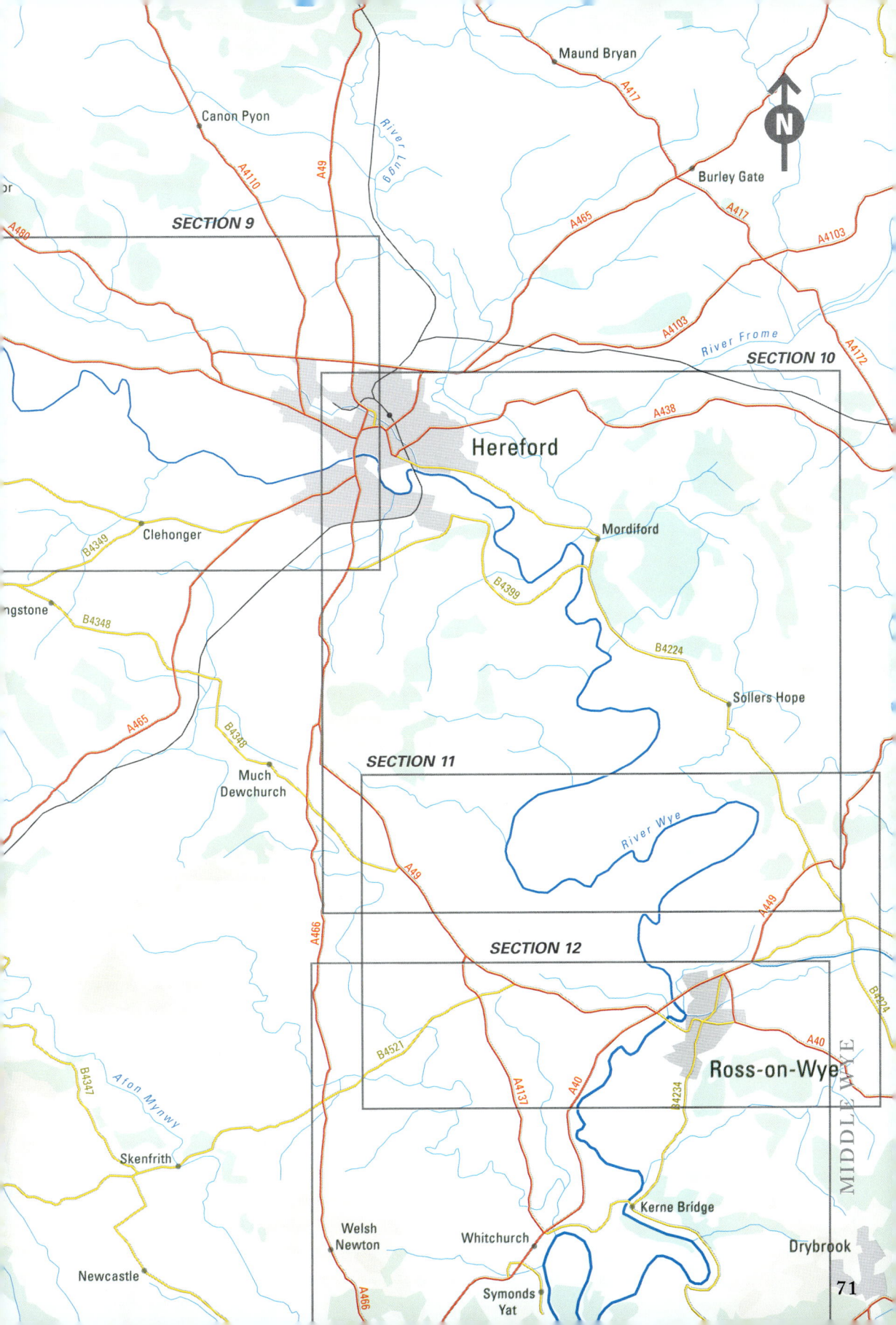

Below Glasbury.

Whitney Bridge.

Section 7

Glasbury to Whitney Bridge

Distance	16.7km
Start	Glasbury SO 179 392 / HR3 5NW
Finish	Whitney Bridge SO 259 475 / HR3 6EW
Difficulty	Grade 1 and 2

Introduction

Justly popular as one of the finest trips on the Wye, this is a unique stretch of untamed winding river with many mildly-challenging rapids and a stunning backdrop of the Black Mountains to savour.

Launch points

Glasbury Bridge SO 179 392 / HR3 5NW – a small car park outside the scout hut, upstream of the bridge on river left. The river is reached through a gate. Launching here was temporarily banned in 2021, see boxed text on page 65 for details.

Hay-on-Wye SO 229 427 / HR3 5BJ – a small car park with steps to the river, on river right downstream of Hay Bridge.

Whitney Bridge SO 259 475 / HR3 6EW – steps lead to the water from the river left bank, upstream of the bridge. A fee is payable to the toll bridge owners.

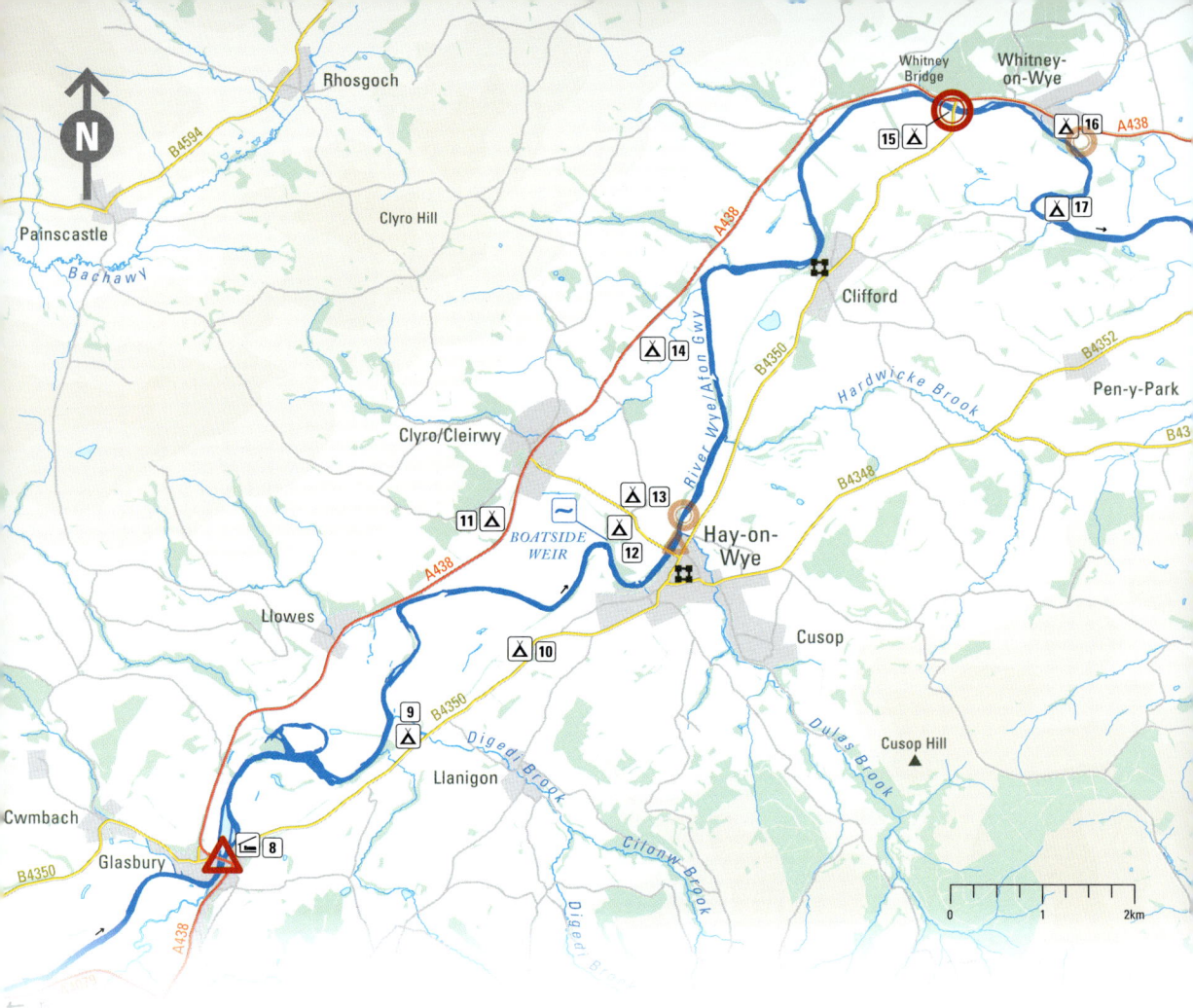

Nearby attractions

The bookshops of Hay-on-Wye are well worth a browse! To the south of town, several Black Mountains summits can easily be accessed by walking or mountain biking from Gospel Pass.

Accommodation

The following campsites are beside the river: Digeddi Wildlife Camping, Racquety Farm, The Pound (behind the Boat Inn, Whitney), Whitney Toll Bridge. The following campsites are nearby: Radnors End Campsite, Ashbrook Caravans and Camping, Black Mountain View. There is a 'posh bunkhouse' belonging to Wye Valley Canoes at Glasbury, and Baskerville Hall Hotel offers camping and 'dorm' accommodation. B&B and hotel information can be obtained from the tourist information centre in Brecon on 01874 622485, and Hay-on-Wye Tourist Information Bureau on 01497 820144.

Description

"The valley widens, the background softens, and the whole scene assumes the character of an English vale." (Leigh Ritchie, *The Wye: A Picturesque Ramble* 1841).

Various information sources and tour operators cite Glasbury as being exactly 100 miles upstream of the muddy take-out on the tidal shore at Chepstow. To be boringly pedantic, the distance is actually 162.3 km, or 101.4 miles … but '100' undeniably has a cooler ring to it.

This section can become rather shallow in places, especially in late summer; loaded boats may occasionally find themselves grounding. Conversely, this section is not to be recommended in high water, as there are many tight turns where the current flows towards bushes and low hanging branches.

The parking area beside Glasbury Scout Hut and public toilets is always a bustling spot, with groups coming and going carrying gear from the scout hut to the river. The scout hut was opened in 1920 by Lord Baden-Powell himself, and is the oldest in Wales still in use. A gate leads to the river's wide gravelly flood plain and in summer it can be a bit of a trek to reach the actual water! You launch directly upstream of Glasbury Bridge, which has carried the A438 since it was built in 1923, being widened twice in the interim. The buildings on river right directly below the bridge are the base of Wye Valley Canoes; you won't fail to notice the huge, stacked pyramid of open canoes awaiting hire! If you are peckish, note The River Café, which they also run.

Crowded craft at Hay-on-Wye.

The river braids around an overgrown island, directly below the bridge. With this and most such islands on this section, resist the temptation to take the narrower channel, should there be sufficient water – it is overgrown and often blocked by fallen trees or branches.

A glance at the map will reveal how the Wye sprawls, braids and meanders unhindered across the plain in the following kilometres. You might be reminded of your school geography lessons! The red earth banks are being actively eroded on the outside of bends; take care not to get swept into overhanging trees and bushes. Look out for remains of a past castle's motte (artificial earth hill) hidden on the river left bank, after 2km.

Over the next few kilometres of small rapids, take time to look back and enjoy the open views of the Black Mountains, which rise steeply to a lofty ridge overlooking the valley; the two prominent peaks are Hay Bluff (677m) and Lord Hereford's Knob (690m). When the river bends left along a wooded slope on the right, you have reached the border of the Brecon Beacons National Park, which follows the river for the next 2km. Another bend, this time to the right, hides a surprise; Boatside Weir, at Wyecliff. This pebble weir is quite harmless (and indeed washes out to become indiscernible in high water), usually being paddled via the exhilarating chute alongside the river right bank.

The kilometre-long bend leading to Hay Bridge passes the campsite of the Hay Festival on the river left bank; in May you will see their 'glamping' tents erected.

Hay Bridge (built 1957) is unusually high, towering above a multi-channelled rapid, the site of a long-ago collapsed weir. The town is to the right, and the right channel leads beneath the bridge to a landing stage and car park which is heavily used by hire operators and outdoor centres. Landing to stretch legs and explore Hay-on-Wye is recommended; note however that it's a steep walk uphill!

For 6km from Hay as far as Rhydspence, the Wye forms the border between Wales and England; paddle along the bank which best suits your national prejudices!

The first sight of note below Hay is the stone ruins of Clifford Castle, looming on river right. This was built after the Norman Conquest for William FitzOsbern, the newly planted Earl of Hereford. It was destroyed in 1402 by the forces of the mysterious Welsh insurgent, Owain Glyndwr, who also destroyed the motte and bailey castle at nearby Hay.

Look out for the Inn at Rhydspence, above on river left. This inn dates right back to the 14th century, and was used for shoeing drover's cattle during their journey from Mid Wales to market in London, and is sometimes called the 'first house in England'.

Whitney Bridge is unmistakeable. This peculiar construction dates from 1802, with two stone arches and three wooden spans; the stone parts survive from before the 1795 flood. This is one of the few privately owned

📷 *Black Mountains from below Glasbury.*

📷 *Lunch stop below Glasbury.*

[◉] *Boatside Weir above Hay.*

toll bridges left in the country. You might also spot the site of another bridge just upstream, which carried a now-dismantled tramway.

The Town of Books

Hay is famous as 'The Town of Books'. This small town, located where the borders of Radnor, Brecon and Herefordshire meet, gained its modern *raison d'etre* from Robert Booth. Owner of Booth Books and the self-styled 'King of Hay', in 1961 he had the inspired idea of promoting Hay as a sort of literary Mecca. Hay became the largest second-hand book selling centre in the world; there are currently over 20 bookshops and over a million books in Hay, although their trade has taken some knocks of late due to the impact of Amazon.com. In 1988 the first Hay Festival of Literature was held, and this is now a major international event running for ten days each May.

[◉] *Playing on Boatside Weir*

Below Bredwardine.

Section 8

Whitney Bridge to Bycross

Distance 20.7km
Start Whitney Bridge SO 259 475 / HR3 6EW
Finish Byecross Farm SO 376 426 / HR2 9LJ
Difficulty Grade 1, possibly one grade 2 rapid

Introduction

This is a lovely paddle, winding past varied rural scenery through a quiet corner of Herefordshire. There is almost no intrusion from the outside world. The flow is slow but there are occasional rapids and riffles to entertain you.

Launch points

Whitney Bridge SO 259 475 / HR3 6EW – steps lead to the water from the river left bank, upstream of the bridge. A fee is payable to the toll bridge owners.

Whitney-on-Wye SO 269 472 / HR3 6EH - Steps on river left leading to car park beside the Boat Inn. Landing generally welcomed, to customers. Launching only with prior permission from the Boat Inn – park and launch beside the Boat Inn on the river left bank.

Bredwardine Bridge SO 336 447 / HR3 6BT – Very limited parking in a layby on river left. Access the river from the footpath on river right, follow it downstream until the bank isn't too steep.

Byecross Farm SO 376 426 / HR2 9LJ – steps and a canoe ramp lead up to the campsite entrance.

Nearby attractions

A steep walk up Merbach Hill offers a fine viewpoint of the Middle Wye's open valley. Brobury House Gardens are right beside Bredwardine Bridge, a great spot for a picnic.

Accommodation

The following campsites are beside the river: The Pound (behind the Boat Inn, Whitney), Oakfield Farm (just past Locksters Pool), The Weston (above Turner's Boat), Byecross Farm. B&B and hotel information can be obtained from Visit Herefordshire 01432 268430, and Hay-on-Wye Tourist Information Bureau on 01497 820144.

Description

Below Whitney Bridge, the river splits around an island with a riffly rapid, one of several such rapids which speed your passage down to the Boat Inn at Whitney-on-Wye. The church at Whitney-on-Wye dates from around 1740, replacing its predecessor which was washed away by a flood in 1735. This flood also removed the rectory and much of the village; looking at the height of the land above the water, this is almost impossible to imagine.

Launching from the Boat Inn, the flow initially carries you swiftly alongside a long island. Henceforth, key characteristics of this section are the subtlest of riffles, interspersed with slow deep pools; the first pool encountered is Locksters Pool, on a left bend. Here, in 1927,

Rapid upstream of Bredwardine Bridge.

Paddleboarder near Bycross.

the largest salmon ever rod-caught in British waters (27 kilos!) was hooked out by Mrs Doreen Davey.

The field on river right after Locksters Pool Farm is a campsite. The author has watched otters playing here, early one morning.

The next ten kilometres are some of the most benign on the whole river, allowing you to drift and soak up the scenery. Merbach Hill rises directly from the river right bank to a 318m summit, before you pass by Turner's Boat Island, an overgrown and swampy tangle of channels. The distinctive hefty-sized cows quietly watching your passage with red coats and white faces and markings are, of course, the locally bred Hereford Cattle. These supposedly produce the finest beef in world; herds were introduced to the USA around 1816, and also shipped down to Argentina, from whence they have returned to the UK as tins of corned beef.

When the river bends sharp right with trees on both banks, brace yourself for a sudden wake-up. Bedrock slabs funnel the flow to the inside of the bend, causing a notable rapid … well, it feels notable enough after ten kilometres of flat water! Be alert, as the current trends towards bushes and overhanging trees.

Bredwardine Bridge is 600m past the rapid, perhaps the most attractive bridge on the whole river. Six red brick arches arc high above the flow; its height is perhaps why it was the first bridge along the river to survive the 1795 flood. It was built in 1769 as a toll bridge on the site of a former ferry. It's not quite as authentic as it first seems though, having been rebuilt in its original form in 1922. If you don't mind a slippery scramble to the footpath on river right, it is possible to visit the gardens of the Victorian Brobury House, directly across the bridge.

Byecross.

As you paddle past Bredwardine, note the earthen remains of a motte and bailey castle on river right, located here to control the river crossing. The river is now hemmed in by dense foliage on both sides. After adjusting to a world of greenery, it's a bit of a jolt when

Bredwardine Bridge.

Brobury Scar.

the red sandstone cliffs of Brobury Scar are reached, after several kilometres. Called 'The Scar' on OS maps, these loom 50m above a long, right bend. At water level, a rapid speeds your passage, with angular sandstone blocks disrupting the flow. Nonetheless, your eyes will most likely be inclined upwards at the undermined beech trees hanging precariously over the precipice, roots reaching into space. Directly ahead is Moccas Court, an impressive 18th-century brick mansion. The name Moccas comes from the Welsh *moch rhos* (swine heath!), perhaps inappropriate for a Grade 1 listed building, built from a design by Robert Adam, with gardens laid out by Lancelot 'Capability' Brown. Nowadays it is a very expensive hotel. Just past the mansion is the site of a former toll bridge built 1867–9 by Sir Velters Cornewall (of Moccas Court). This was removed after being damaged in a 1960 flood.

After a placid kilometre floating past orchards, the Wye bends left in front of some private houses; at the end of the bend on river right is the landing platform at Byecross Farm Campsite.

Monnington Falls.

📷 *The Weir.*

Below Byford.

Section 9

Bycross to Hereford

Distance 19.7km
Start Byecross Farm SO 376 426 / HR2 9LJ
Finish Hereford SO 509 396 / HR4 9DW
Difficulty Grade 1, one grade 2 rapid

Introduction

The Wye maintains its winding course through beautiful farmland, with highlights including the rapids of Monnington Falls and the gardens at The Weir. Hereford, the only city on the Wye, is a surprisingly pleasant intrusion.

Launch points

Byecross Farm campsite SO 376 426 / HR2 9LJ – steps and a canoe ramp lead to the water from the site entrance.

Byford SO 400 425 / HR4 7LD – an overgrown track leads to the water, from the end of a narrow single-track lane. This spot is little used, as there is nowhere to turn a vehicle, let alone park.

Hereford Rowing Club SO 506 395 / HR4 0BE - steps to the water, long-stay parking possible.

Hereford SO 509 396 / HR4 9DW – take out on the river right bank, in the park shortly after Wye Bridge (the old stone bridge). Wye Street car park is nearby.

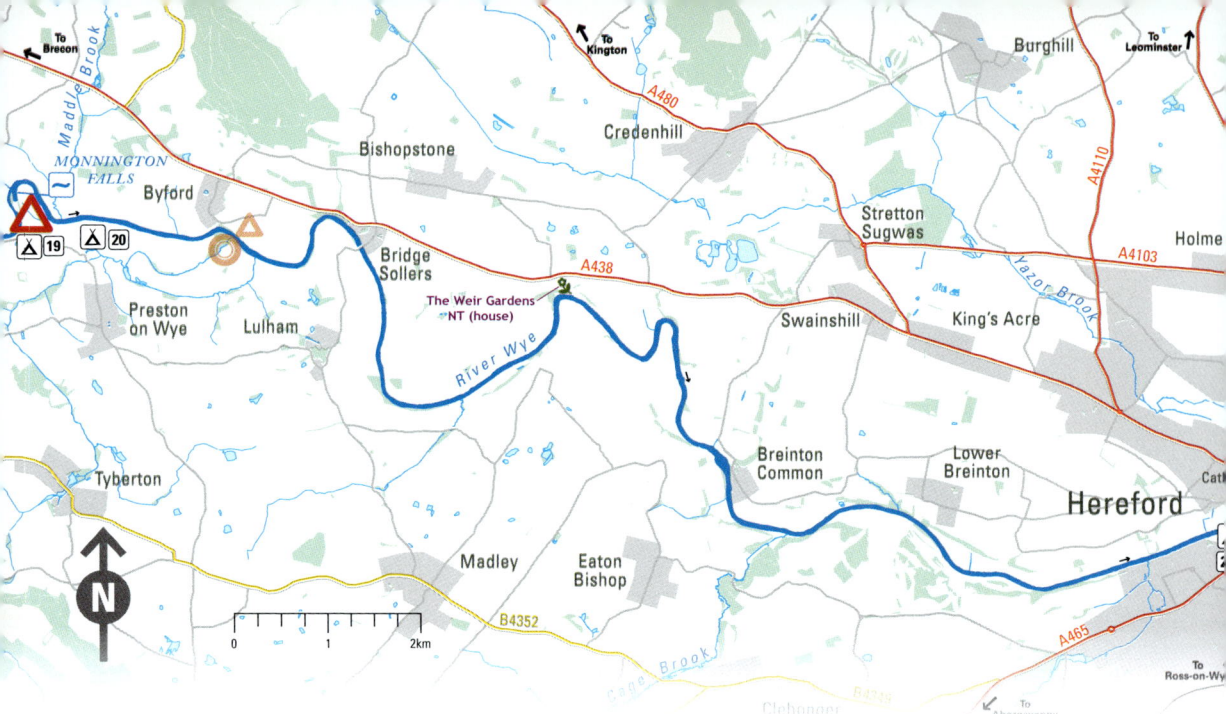

Nearby attractions

Hereford's Waterworks Museum, Byford Church, Hereford Cathedral and The Weir Gardens are referred to below, being accessible from the river. See the boxed text for more information on Hereford's attractions.

Accommodation

The following campsites are beside the river: Byecross Farm, Wyecamphere (Preston Court), and Hereford Rowing Club. B&B and hotel information can be obtained from Visit Herefordshire, 01432 268430.

Description

Byecross Farm Campsite is an idyllic spot to stay (bank holiday weekends excepted), should you have the time. The regimented lines of trees that you pitch your tent beneath are a typical Herefordshire cider apple orchard. Local varieties include 'Handsome Norman' and 'Hagloe Crab', and the cider produced from these apples is exported, to be consumed in inadvisable quantities, worldwide.

Directly after launching, you are confronted with one of the few horizon lines on the English Wye. This is Monnington Falls, but don't panic, it isn't a 'fall' as such. Approaching carefully along the river left bank, you will see that a series of wide, shallow-angled bedrock reefs interrupt the river's course. In high water, the reefs simply submerge and there are just a few waves here. In medium water levels, various rocky routes are possible down the face of the slabs – fun, but proceed with care! In low summer levels, the slabs are left high and dry, and the only paddling option is to follow the deep boily channel which bypasses the slabs by flowing to the left of an island.

The channel is narrow and can be blocked by low branches or even fallen trees, so inspect first by landing and walking down the river left bank.

Historically, Monnington Falls was the main obstacle to river trade and commerce upstream of Hereford. The *Rivers Wye and Lugg Navigation Act* of 1695 attempted to clear the river to allow barges upriver, but twenty years later complaints were made that an eight-foot high stone weir was still barring passage at Monnington! This is possibly the origin of the 'Falls' name. Paddlers will be relieved (or disappointed?) that no trace of this remains today. Once the weir was demolished, barges did manage to pass through en route to destinations as far upstream as Hay, laboriously unloading their cargo and hauling the barge up the reefs using pulleys and a fixed windlass.

Monnington-on-Wye is hidden from view a few hundred metres back on river left, but is worthy of mention as the place where 15th-century Welsh insurgent Owain Glyndwr reputedly died. After many years of fighting wars against English overlordship, Glyndwr vanished from public view. Despite the offer of huge rewards, Glyndwr was never betrayed by his fellow countrymen and his whereabouts in his later years are a complete mystery.

At the start of a 2km straight, the church of Preston Court village is visible on river right, as you pass the Wyecamphere campsite.

When the river winds past several houses on the left, the village of Byford has been reached. This was once the site of a ferry and ford. As the last houses are passed, hidden beneath low-hanging trees on river left is a track which leads up to the village, a possible launch or landing point. Byford's small church originates from the 11th century. In 1951, renovations uncovered previously unsuspected 14th-century wall paintings, which can be viewed by visitors.

A right bend crosses the line of Offa's Dyke, the border of Early Medieval Wales, which was clearly larger than today. Around this bend is a concrete bridge. The village on the left is Bridge Sollars, but peculiarly this name predates any bridges, being Scandinavian in origin.

A quiet 4km brings paddlers to a small rapid leading towards a stone pier on the river left bank of a right bend, beneath terraced orna-

A Royal Record

In 1846, a local man thought he glimpsed a large salmon in a shady pool at The Weir. He entered the water and attempted to wrestle the fish ashore. After an epic fight, he landed the 'salmon', which turned out to be an 8.5 foot, 185lb royal sturgeon, almost unheard of in British waters.

mental gardens. These make quite a change from the rural landscapes encountered hitherto! This is 'The Weir', a National Trust property. Steps lead up to the gardens, which are open to visitors; hopefully you brought your membership card! There is a 'tea tent' consisting solely of a self-service machine, rather disappointing for those who associate the NT with teapots and Victoria sponge. The gardens are a lovely place to explore however, especially in the spring when snowdrops and daffodils make their appearance. There hasn't been a weir here since the 17th century. The origins of the site are much older; excavations along the bank have discovered remains of a substantial Roman building, either a villa or a temple with direct access to the Wye. A Roman road once bridged the Wye just 1km downstream, and less than a kilometre north is the site of the Roman town of *Magna Castra*. The river takes a sharp bend to the south below the sandstone Weir Cliff (again, no weir survives today) and passes several villages in succession. A rapid alongside an island first leads to Breinton Common on river left, and then Ruckhall on river right. The steep slope rising behind Ruckhall is Eaton Camp, an Iron Age hill fort. The third village is Lower Breinton on river left, recognised by the spire of Breinton Church. The 18th-century Belmont House (now a hotel and golf course) is passed on the right, and then a pumping station on a left bend reveals a 2.5km near-straight section of river leading into Hereford. Watch out for the rowers who frequent this stretch.

As you pass the houses of Hunderton on river right, on the river left bank is the Waterworks Museum, within a Victorian water pumping

Hereford

The city's name is Old English: *here* (soldiers) and *ford* (crossing). If exploring ashore, the 14th-century cathedral is the most obvious draw. A donation is invited from those visiting. Highlights include the Chained Library which contains 1500 books and manuscripts dating back to the 8th century, and the remarkable *Mappa Mundi*, a medieval map of the world preserved on vellum. During the 18th and 19th centuries, Hereford was a centre for boatbuilding and river trade. Cider was a key 'export', shipped downriver to Bristol. The Cider Museum will appeal to those with an unhealthy fascination for this drink! In 1845, the Herefordshire and Gloucester Canal was opened, reducing river traffic. The canal in turn was soon made obsolete by the 1855 opening of the Hereford, Ross and Gloucester Railway. Hereford still remembers the importance of the Wye with an annual River Festival. The Three Choirs Festival, the oldest music festival in Europe, also takes place here every three years.

Hereford is also famous as the home of the SAS Regiment, which is based at Credenhill. The Special Air Service is the British Army's elite special forces unit.

◯ *The Weir.*

station. The first bridge passed beneath is Hunderton Bridge, a 1912–13 railway bridge which is now used by walkers and cyclists. Then follows busy Greyfriars Bridge, the main road crossing in Hereford since its construction in 1966. Directly after are the stone arches of the 15th-century Wye Bridge, the oldest bridge still surviving on the Wye. Hereford Cathedral's red-brown sandstone pinnacled tower rises directly behind, marking the end of your trip. Just after Wye Bridge, the Bishop's Palace is visible in front of the cathedral on river left, and there are various landing options on river right. In summer, look for the white flowers of crowfoot growing across the river here; crowfoot thrives in gravel, especially sites disturbed by manmade works – this was the site of an ancient ford.

Hereford.

Carey Islands.

Section 10

Hereford to Hoarwithy

Distance	25.3km
Start	Hereford SO 509 396 / HR4 9DW
Finish	Hoarwithy SO 548 292 / HR2 6QH
Difficulty	Grade 1

Introduction

The paddle out of Hereford is a slow start, but the scenery improves dramatically as the Wye reaches the uplands of Woolhope Dome. It then winds across a wide plain from one steep hillside to another, in little hurry to make progress south.

Launch points

Hereford SO 509 396 / HR4 9DW – launch on the river right bank, in the park shortly after Wye Bridge (the old stone bridge). Wye Street car park is nearby.

Lucksall Caravan and Camping Park SO 568 363 / HR1 4LP – a launching fee is payable at reception. Launch from the steps at the far end of the site.

Hoarwithy SO 548 292 / HR2 6QH – land at the campsites located about 300m below Hoarwithy Bridge; there are campsites on both banks, Tresseck Farm (river right) is closest to the village.

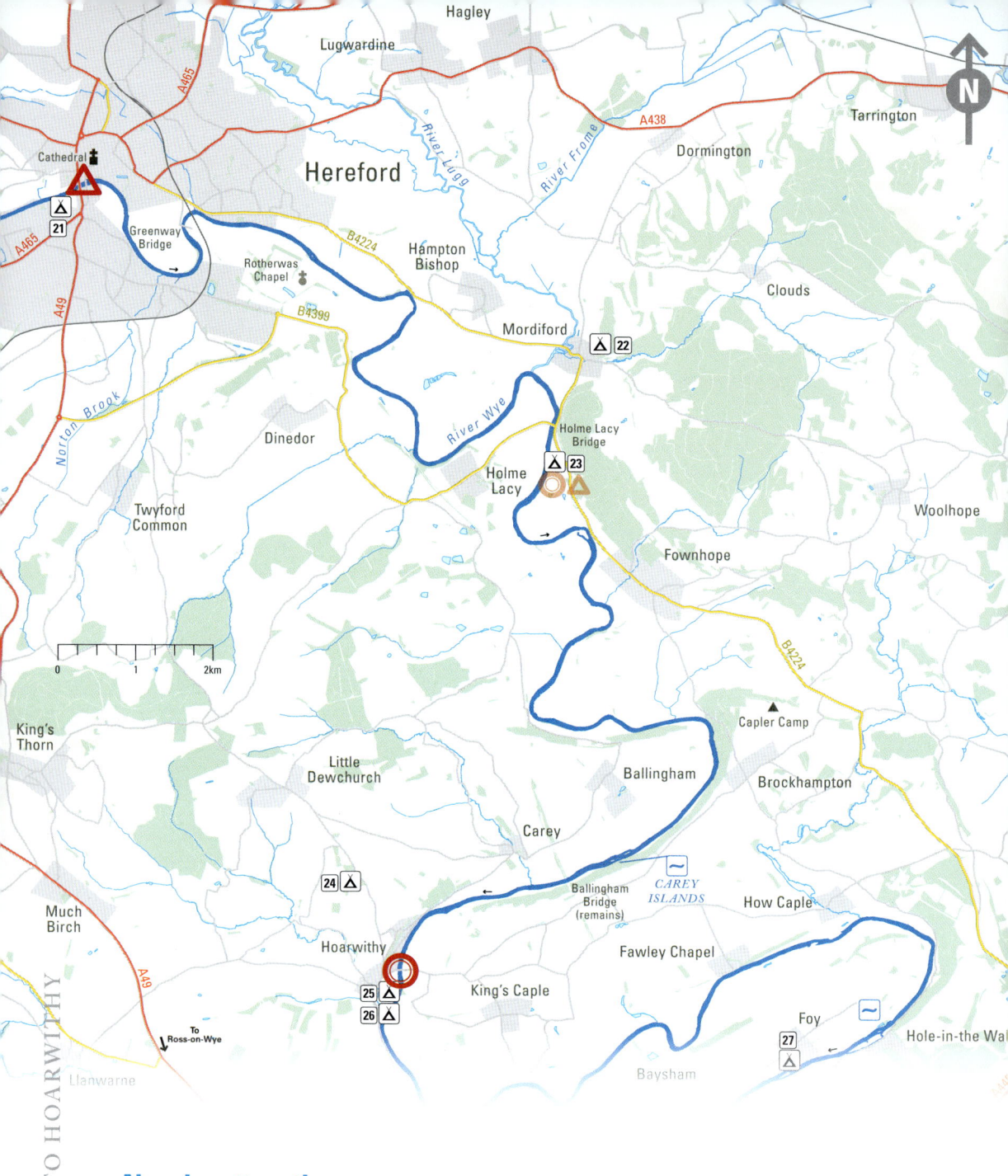

Nearby attractions

Rotherwas Chapel is mentioned below. Sufton Court is a 1788 mansion at Mordiford, overlooking the confluence of the Wye and the Lugg. Walkers, and especially naturalists, will enjoy exploring the hills and meadows of Woolhope Dome, the high ground stretching east from the Wye.

Accommodation

The following campsites are beside the river: Hereford Rowing Club, Lucksall Caravan and Camping Park (below Holme Lacy Bridge), Lower Ruxton Farm 01432 840223 Tresseck Farm. The following campsites are nearby: The Moon Inn is at Mordiford, and Woodland Tipi and Yurts near Hoarwithy offer glamping. B&B and hotel information can be obtained from Visit Herefordshire 01432 268430.

Description

"A range of hills called Capler Hills form a rich screen to the northern bank of the Wye ... the soil has a reddish cast and gives a warm and animated tinge to the landscape." (Samuel Ireland, *Picturesque Views on the River Wye* 1797) Launch downstream of Wye Bridge, opposite

Hereford Cathedral.

Hereford. Cathedral.

the Cathedral and Bishop's Palace. Just below is Victoria Bridge, a footbridge built in 1897 to commemorate Queen Victoria's Diamond Jubilee. It links two public parks; the King George V Playing Field on river right, and the Castle Green on river left. Castle Green (which has a 'Nelson Column') is perched on a mound, the former site of Hereford Castle. This was built c. 1070, one of a chain of border castles constructed along the Wye for Norman overlord William FitzOsbern. The already dilapidated castle was captured by Parliament in 1645 during the Civil War and dismantled.

The Wye winds its way out of Hereford over the following 4km, with the banks mostly shielding the housing from view. Unfortunately there is no ignoring the foamy outflows from two different sewage works which discharge who-knows-what into the river.

After passing beneath a bridge of industrial pipes, the Greenway Bridge is reached, the Wye's newest crossing. This gleaming white suspension footbridge was built in 2013 at a cost of £3 million, and hence possibly won't appear on your OS map. Shortly after is Eign Railway Bridge, which should be on your map, as it's been there since 1931. About 1.6km further on river right is medieval Rotherwas Chapel, formerly the family chapel of the Roman Catholic Bodenham family and now managed by English Heritage.

A sharp right bend in front of a high flood bank is the sign that you have finally escaped Hereford. Across the bank on river left is the village of Hampton Bishop, where the 'Bunch of Carrots' pub is named after one of the Wye's salmon pools. The raised bank continues along the left shore for about 4km, to where a small rocky rapid leads down to the confluence of the River Lugg, the Wye's largest English tributary. The village of Mordiford with its nine-arched bridge is a few hundred metres upstream, should you fancy a diversion.

Henceforth and until the River Severn is reached, you are within the Wye Valley Area of Outstanding Natural Beauty (AONB). The hills of Woolhope Dome close in on the left, indeed for the rest of this trip you are either

Woolhope Dome

The range of hills along the river left bank of the Wye from Mordiford to Capler Camp is known as Woolhope Dome. Many of the hills are cloaked in fields of wildflowers and ancient oak woodlands. Naturalists value this region for the diversity of flora and fauna; the fertility of the terrain is a result of the Silurian limestones and sandstones that underlay the hills, the oldest rocks in the Wye Valley AONB. The Wye's wide meanders below Hereford can be explained by the relative softness of these rocks. The rocks have eroded back to form wide valley sides, then being spread as river alluvium, creating the fertile red and brown soils of Herefordshire.

Approaching Holme Lacy Bridge.

alongside a steep, wooded slope or heading towards one!

Holme Lacy Bridge dates from the 1970s, on the site of a Victorian toll bridge and an earlier ferry. Shortly below on the river left bank is Lucksall Caravan and Camping Park, which has a launch or landing point at the far end. Hereford Canoe Hire have a base here, and you will usually encounter other paddlers splashing about.

Fownhope is the large village visible on river left, 2km further on. A footpath leads to the village, which has a shop and other facilities. Fownhope is peculiar in that it still celebrates Apple Oak Day, 29th May. This commemorates the Restoration of King Charles II in 1660 (on his birthday, mine too, but I digress) and involves the wearing of oak apples to commemorate Charles' hiding in an oak tree to escape his Parliamentary pursuers during the Civil War. This public holiday was abolished in 1859, but no one seems to have told the people of Fownhope.

Capler Camp overlooks a right bend of the Wye, rising 140m upwards from the water. Obscured in the trees at the summit is a large bivallate (i.e. double-walled) Iron Age hill fort. Past the hill fort, the wooded slopes continue along the river left bank for about 4km, this being one of the most attractive stretches of the whole river. You might glimpse overgrown quarries which yielded stone for Hereford

Hoarwithy.

Cathedral. At early morning, deer emerge from the woods and scramble down to the river to drink. Reaching Carey Wood with the Carey Islands alongside, it's hard to visualise this as the industrial site it once was, but the river left bank was formerly the ironworks of Carey Mills, and a weir provided the power source for the bellows. Today, the Carey Islands are idyllic; the three long islands are covered with alder trees and stretch for 500m along the river. The current rushes around them forming small rapids; pick the route which suits you best!

You may see tents in the field on river right after the islands. This is not a public campsite; however it is sometimes used for church camps and suchlike.

Shortly after the islands, you are confronted with the sight of five towering stone pillars, three of which rise directly from the river. This striking location is Ballingham Bridge, a dismantled railway viaduct. The Wye then gradually bends left, the start of two vast loops it completes before Ross-on-Wye. Houses, and the road along the river right bank, indicate your arrival at Hoarwithy; the village's name is Old English for the whitebeam tree. Hoarwithy Bridge is a modern construction, and from here it's just 300m down to the campsites on both banks; choose your take-out. River left is Lower Ruxton Farm. River right (Tresseck Farm) is obviously closer to the village centre, which includes the New Harp Inn which doubles as the village shop, and the remarkable St Catherine's Church.

St Catherine's

The church at Hoarwithy is quite unlike anything else in Britain. A visit is recommended, especially as it isn't clear just how unique it is until you get up close. Rendered in local sandstone, the architectural style is a hybrid of Italianate, Byzantine and Romanesque; basically, it wouldn't look out of place on a Mediterranean hillside. Steep steps lead up to a tall campanile square tower with a pointed roof. Beneath, a Romanesque cloister catches the light of the setting sun, while the interior borrows styles from France and Italy. The oil lamps are copies of those in Venice's St Mark's Cathedral and the pulpit models that of Fiesole Cathedral in Florence. Stained glass was made by Edward Burne-Jones and William Morris. There is even a Roman-style hypocaust (heated under-floor)! What is this doing in a tiny Herefordshire village? It was built between 1870 and 1900 on the whim of vicar William Poole, a wealthy aesthete who regarded the previous church as, *"an ugly building with no pretensions to any style of architecture"*, and raised the money himself from property rental. Hoarwithy's remarkable little church has since been used as a location in three different films.

Hereford Cathedral.

Hole-in-the-Wall.

Remains of Backney Bridge.

Section 11

Hoarwithy to Ross-on-Wye

Distance	18.8km
Start	Hoarwithy SO 548 292 / HR2 6QH
Finish	Ross-on-Wye SO 595 241 / HR9 7BT
Difficulty	Grade 1

Introduction

The fact that no road crosses the Wye between Hoarwithy and Ross-on-Wye gives a clue that this section winds across a sleepy backwater of Herefordshire, where traffic is almost non-existent (unless you count tractors) and the settlements are few and tiny. The Wye describes the letter S in two vast loops, meaning that although you paddle nearly 19km, you wind up only 7km from your start point.

Launch points

Hoarwithy SO 548 292 / HR2 6QH – launch from either of the campsites located about 300m below Hoarwithy Bridge; Tresseck Farm (on river right) is closest to the village.

Ross-on-Wye SO 595 241 / HR9 7BT – launch point on river left, 200m past the Hope and Anchor Inn. A path leads across a small park to Wye Street where there is parking.

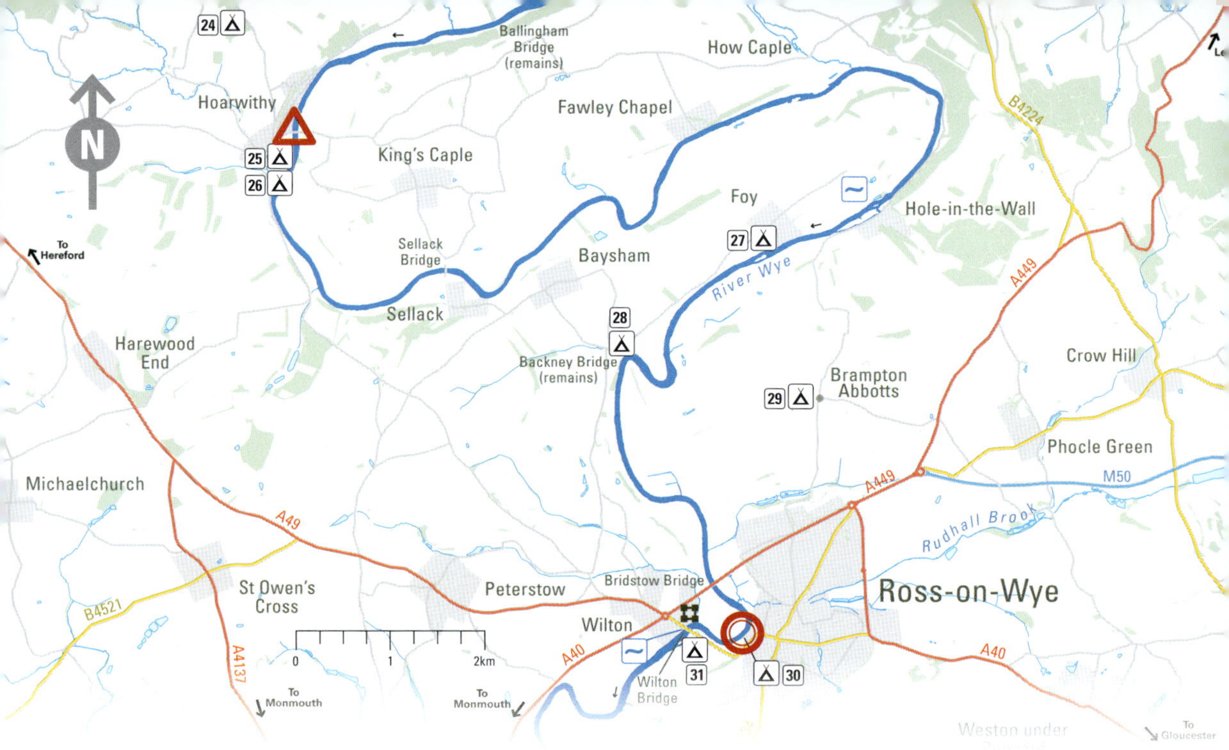

Nearby attractions

A visit to St Catherine's Church in Hoarwithy is a must. Ross-on-Wye is outlined in the boxed text.

◉ *Hole-in-the-Wall.*

Accommodation

The following campsites are beside the river: Tresseck Farm, Lower Ruxton Farm, Martha's Meadow (Foy), Ross Rowing Club, the White Lion Inn. The following campsites are nearby: Backney Bridge, Mad Dogs and Vintage Vans offer glamping at Brampton Abbotts near Ross. B&B and hotel information can be obtained from Visit Herefordshire 01432 268430.

Description

There is nothing much to see along here, and that's what you've come for. Below Hoarwithy, your only company will be the ubiquitous Hereford cattle, the blue-orange flash of the kingfisher, and perhaps the occasional folks fly fishing out in the flow. Attractive wooded

How Caple Wood.

hills are always within view, but mostly do not closely encroach.

After 3km, the spire of St Tysilio's Church in Sellack is visible on river right, and a suspension footbridge is reached. Sellack Bridge connects Sellack with the village of King's Caple. The spot is named Sellack Boat, after a past ferry service. Beneath the footbridge is an inscription: *"To the honour of God and the last union of these parishes"*.

Several kilometres further, the hamlet of Fawley Chapel is seen on river left. There is indeed a Norman chapel here. A long bend to the right brings the Wye alongside the How Caple Wood, which is reminiscent of Capler Camp (section 10) in the way it continues along the river left bank. The river right bank is a private

St Catherine's Church, Hoarwithy.

📷 *Ross-on-Wye.*

estate where no landing will be tolerated, and there are numerous helpful signs to make sure that you do not forget this.

Where the wooded hillside is interrupted by a side valley, several buildings can be seen among the trees. This is the quirkily-named village of Hole-in-the-Wall, and the buildings you see are the home of PGL Travel and their original adventure centre. If you are old enough to remember the 1970s TV series 'Survivors', this is where it was filmed. Several islands and shoals break up the current past Hole-in-the-Wall, forming riffly rapids. These riffles continue alongside the longest island, right down to Foy Bridge.

Foy Bridge is another suspension footbridge, built in 1919 on the site of a ferry, to allow parishioners to reach St Mary's Church in Foy, which is visible downstream on river right. The name incidentally comes from the French for 'faith'. Martha's Meadow is close to the river right bank in Foy, administered by the Camping and Caravanning Club.

Some 2km past the Foy Bridge, the Wye winds around Backney Common. On the left shore, look out for a metal cross honouring the vicar of Brampton Abbotts, who in 1904 drowned while rescuing his son and his daughter's

📷 *'Leaping Salmon' sculpture, Ross-on-Wye.*

Ross-on-Wye

This attractive market town overlooks a loop in the river from a sandstone cliff. Walking uphill from the river, note the Leaping Salmon sculpture outside the Man of Ross pub, the Tudor timbered houses, and the sandstone Market House which was built in 1650. Passing St Mary's Church, look for the Plague Cross which marks a mass grave containing about 300 victims from a 1637 outbreak. Ross hosts an annual Walking Festival in September.

friend. At the end of the common, five tall masonry pillars mark former site of Backney Bridge, almost a facsimile of Ballingham Bridge (section 10).

The Wye has finally decided which direction it wants to head; south towards the spire of St Mary the Virgin, at Ross-on-Wye. The town is a distinctive sight from the river, perched atop a sandstone outcrop. This was formed by the river, which once meandered right around the town. Passing beneath the A40 traffic on Bridstow Bridge, you reach the rowing club on river left, followed by the steps in front of the Hope and Anchor Inn, and then the concrete canoe landing steps.

Fawley Chapel.

Symonds Yat.

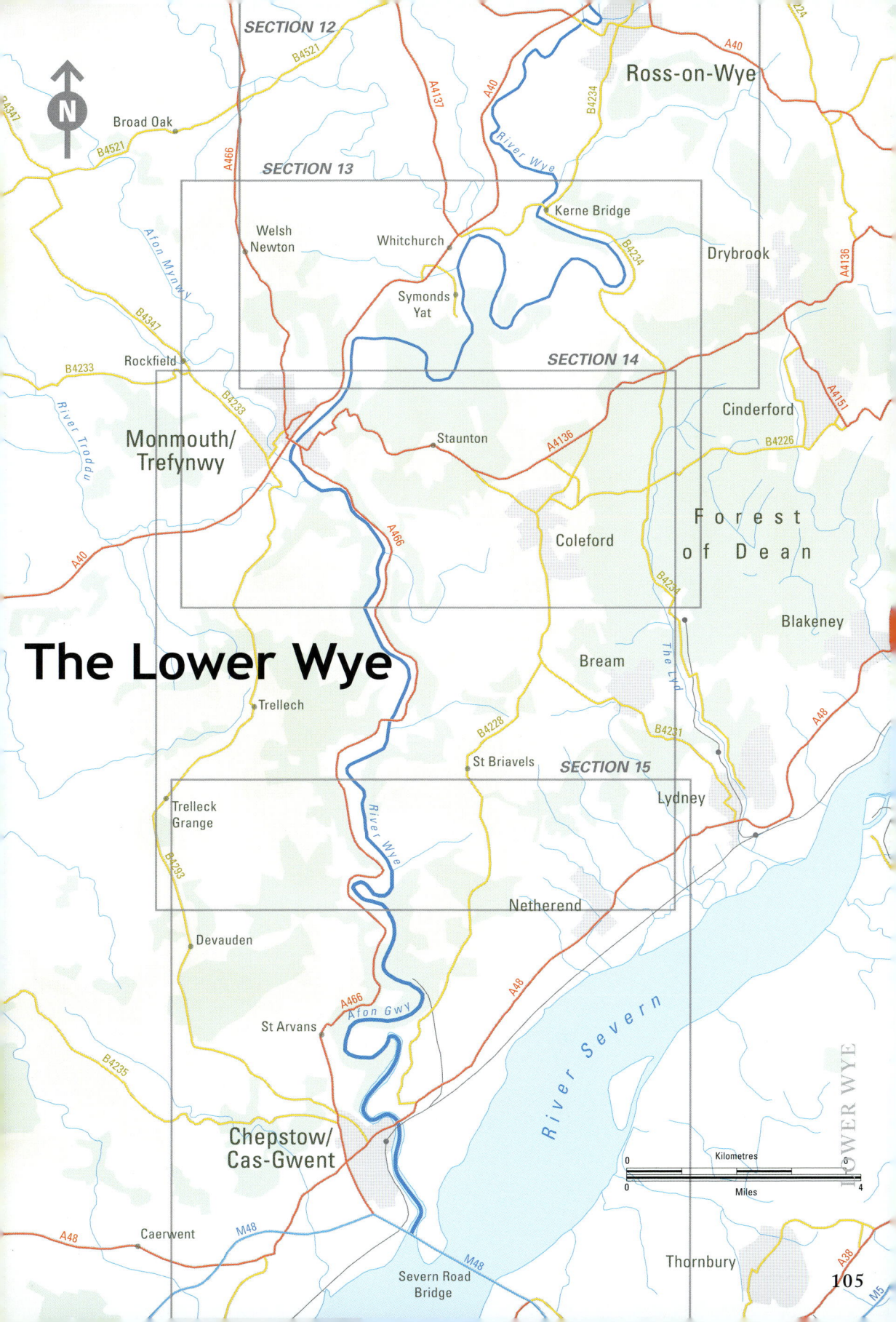

Below Symonds Yat Rock

Lower Lydbrook rapid.

Section 12

Ross-on-Wye to Symonds Yat East

Distance	23.4km
Start	Ross-on-Wye SO 595 241 / HR9 7BT
Finish	Symonds Yat East SO 561 160 / HR9 6BY
Difficulty	Grade 1

Introduction

The Wye carves a route south into the first of its two limestone gorges. Paddlers get to enjoy regular small rapids past hills that progressively steepen, rising eventually to a scenic crescendo as you pass beneath the dramatic Yat Rock. It's not hard to see why this is one of the most popular sections of the Wye.

Launch points

Ross-on-Wye SO 595 241 / HR9 7BT – the launch point is a ramp with wheelchair access on river left, 100m downstream of the Riverside Inn. A path leads from Wye Street (opposite the bandstand) across a small park to the river.

Kerne Bridge SO 582 187 / HR9 5QT – is a large parking and picnic area on river left, 750m

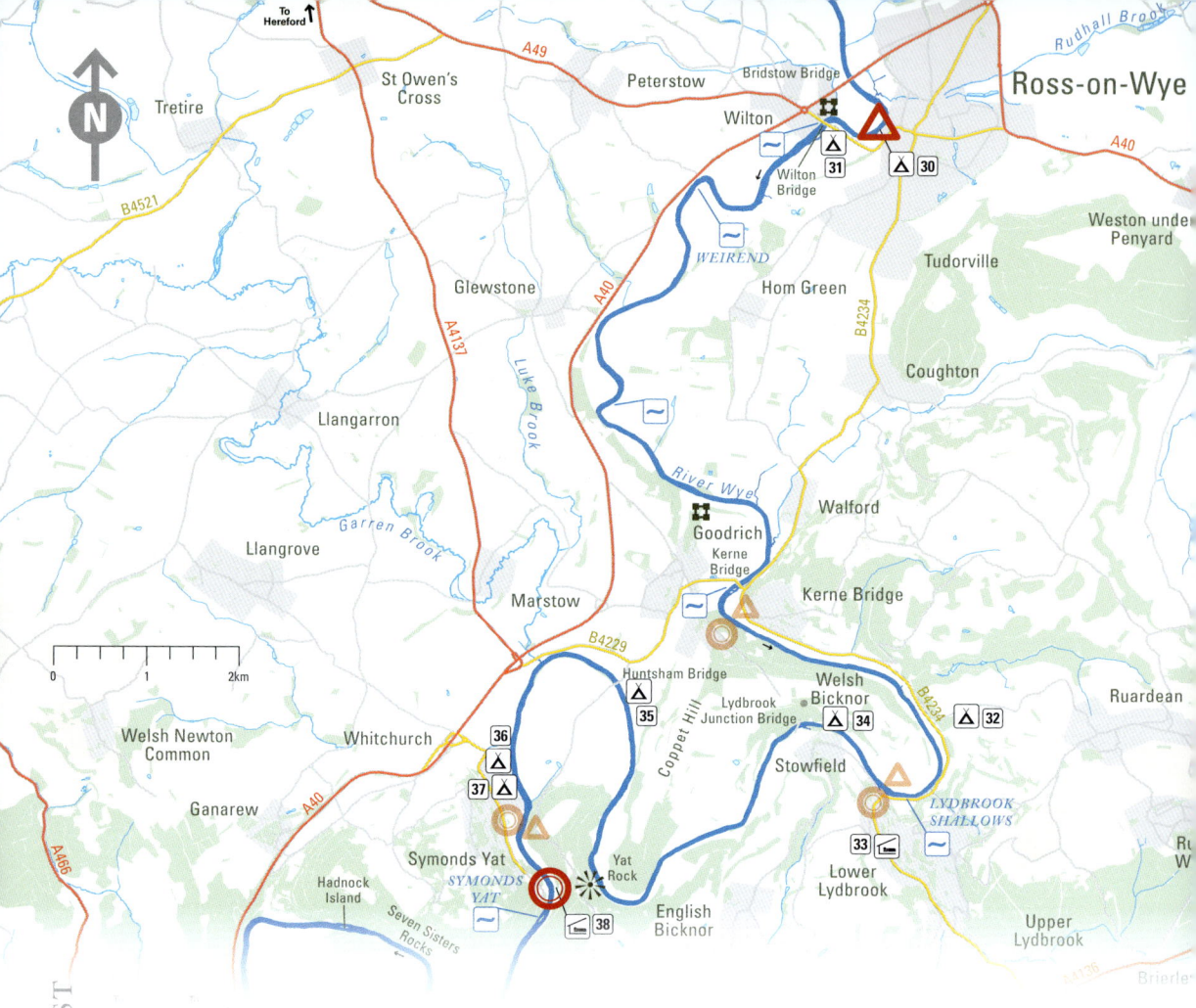

downstream of the bridge along the B4234. Another ramp with wheelchair access.

Lower Lydbrook SO 596 170 / GL17 9NJ – a small honesty box-charged parking area and picnic spot which has steps down to the river on river left. This is not suitable for large groups.

Huntsham Bridge Camping SO 568 181 / HR9 6JN – only with prior arrangement from the campsite, fee payable.

Symonds Yat West SO 557 165 / HR9 6BN– beside Ye Old Ferrie Inn.

Symonds Yat East SO 561 160 / HR9 6BY – the car park belongs to Wyedean Canoe Centre. Disembark at the first set of launching steps reached, beside the seal launch ramp.

Nearby attractions

Goodrich Castle is excellent fun to explore. At Symonds Yat West, two adjacent attractions will keep children entertained; the Butterfly Zoo and the Maze. For walkers, the whole area is a delight. The viewpoint of Yat Rock is one of the finest in the country,

Approaching Kerne Bridge.

accessed by a steep walk from Symonds Yat East, or a short walk from the car park.

Accommodation

The following campsites are beside the river: Ross Rowing Club, The White Lion Inn, Huntsham Bridge Camping, River Wye Camping (Symonds Yat West), and Sterrett's Caravan Park (Symonds Yat West). YHA Wye Valley (Welsh Bicknor) offers riverside camping and is obviously also a hostel. Bunkhouses are found at The Colliers Inn (Lydbrook), Ye Old Ferrie Inn (Symonds Yat West), and Ragmans Farm (Lydbrook) which also offers yurt glamping. B&B and hotel information can be obtained from Visit Herefordshire 01432 268430 and Wyedean Tourism 01594 810000.

Description

"*The banks for the most part rise abruptly from the edge of the water, and are clothed with forests, or broken into cliffs ... The general character of the scenery, is wildness and solitude.*" (William Coxe, *An Historical Tour through Monmouthshire* 1801).

Ross-on-Wye was the usual departure point for 18th and 19th-century visitors taking the famous 'Wye Tour' to Chepstow. The trend for this, Britain's first package holiday, was originated in 1745 when the Vicar of Ross, Dr John Egerton, started taking guests down the Wye. The Wye bends left on leaving Ross, just upstream of Wilton Bridge. This crossing is guarded just upstream by Wilton Castle, visible on river right. The castle originated as a Norman motte and bailey, with sandstone

Kerne Bridge.

walls added later. It was burned down in the Civil War, and the remains later converted into a mansion. It's now a private residence, but is sometimes open to public.

The sandstone bridge dates from the 16th century and also suffered damage in the Civil War. Traces of an 18th-century sundial can be seen, as well as rope marks eroded into the pillars by the hauling of barges, which was often done by humans. Further evidence of the river's commercial past can be seen in the traces of a wharf just downstream of the bridge. The White Lion Inn is on river right, where it is possible to camp. An island just below the bridge is passed to the right, through the first rapid of the day. The waters then quieten down, although unfortunately the A40 is close by and can always be heard for the next few kilometres.

Banks along this stretch are often honeycombed with sand martin burrows. Between March and October you find yourself surrounded by dozens, and often hundreds, of these small birds constantly flitting to and fro across the water, barely missing your boat and paddles.

Two kilometres past Wilton Bridge, a sharp left bend at Weirend hides the longest rapid on this section, a bouncy but mild succession of waves. Weirend rapid was indeed the site of a weir in the 17th century, measuring 2m high. The next rapid is found 3km further on, approaching another sharp left bend, with a prominent white building (the Pencraig Court Hotel) above.

As the river bends away from the A40, the scenery improves, with wooded hills closing in. Goodrich Castle rises above the trees on river right; this was a highlight of the Wye Tour. The attractive stone-arched Kerne Bridge was built in 1828 as a toll bridge. Directly below is a boily rapid where currents converge

Goodrich Castle

This spectacular and well-preserved sandstone castle almost seems to spring out of the ground; perhaps because it was constructed using stone quarried from the moat around it. It originates from the 11th century, unusually dating from before the Norman Conquest. Its name comes from Godric, the English earl who owned it. The Normans added the impressive walls and square keep. During the Civil War, Sir Henry Lingen held Goodrich for the king against a long Parliamentary siege. The castle finally fell in 1646 after a pounding by a huge mortar 'Roaring Meg', on view in the castle today. Parliament ordered for the castle to be "totally disgarrisoned and slighted" but the walls still stand strong. A visit is recommended, however the easiest access for paddlers is from the back, via Kerne Bridge.

beside a gravel bank, below low branches. This has been known to catch paddlers out! The rapid continues past an island into calmer water. This leads to a landing point and picnic area 750m downstream of the bridge on river left, at the site of a former railway bridge.

Kerne Bridge and Huntsham Bridge are less than 2km apart, but the Wye winds for 11km between them, tracing the outline of 188m high Coppet Hill, a nature reserve bought by the community, on river right. From Kerne Bridge, the Wye flows south-east for 3km, passing some static caravans and a water extraction plant before reaching the houses of Lower Lydbrook. A riffly rapid known as Lydbrook Shallows leads past to a launch point and picnic site on river left. It seems inconceivable

📷 *Goodrich Castle, Roaring Meg cannon.*

📷 *Lydbrook Shallows.*

that this almost idyllic spot was until recent times an industrial hub. The steep brook powered coal mines, tin plate works, wire works, and iron forges; the first commercial blast furnace operated here from 1608. Lydbrook Shallows was the site of a wharf to load coal onto barges headed to Hereford. A 30m railway viaduct towered overhead (built 1873, demolished 1965) spanning the Lydbrook valley.

At Lydbrook, the Wye reaches strata of harder Carboniferous limestone, and is deflected 180 degrees away to the north-west. The hamlet of Welsh Bicknor (which is not in Wales) is passed, recognisable by the attractive tower of St Margaret's Church. If staying at the youth hostel here, it's possible to moor and land. Some 400m further are the grim black metal tubes of Lydbrook Junction Bridge, on which are painted faded safety instructions to canoeists; if you can read them, you are probably too close! The railway which crossed here was closed in 1964, it is now a footbridge. In the trees on river left, you will catch glimpses of old factory buildings. This site produced the telephone cables used in the trenches of the First World War, which explains the presence of the pillbox on the river right side of the bridge.

The Wye bends back to the south-west and approaches the limestone area once more. This time it cuts into the limestone, forming a line of vertical cliffs: *"Approaching the foot of Coldwell Rocks, a most sublime and majestic scene presents itself."* (Thomas Roscoe, *Wanderings and Excursions in South Wales* c. 1839). Wye Tourists like Roscoe would

Symonds Yat East launch point.

View from Symonds Yat Rock.

disembark here, to be guided up the cliffs to the viewpoint of Symonds Yat Rock 120m above, and then down the far side of the hill to Symonds Yat East, just 400m away but 6km downstream around Huntsham Hill. Paddlers gazing up today will spy the milling tourists and flagpole at Yat Rock. Many of these folk will actually be birdwatchers hoping to catch a glimpse of the peregrine falcons which nest in Coldwell Rocks. They are well established now, but the arrival of the first pair in 1982 (after an absence of decades) was the cause of national celebration. Yat Rock was the site of an Iron Age hill fort, which must have been of some importance, having no fewer than four lines of earth walls.

The Wye is deflected northwards once more, away from the resistant limestone and (temporarily) clear of the enclosing hills. Huntsham Bridge, a 1982 metal construction, is passed beneath, before the river bends south at Old Forge. About 150m inland on river left is the wind and rain-eroded Queen Stone, one of the few Neolithic standing stones in the region. At Whitchurch, the first landing stage you see on river right, is a campsite. Shortly below is Symonds Yat West, always a bustle of activity. You will see *Wye Pride* and *Kingfisher* chugging up and down, the two tour boats of 'Kingfisher Cruises'. At the Ye Old Ferrie Inn, a hand-powered chain ferry operates to take walkers across the river. Note also hereabouts, a large rock on river left which is popular for jumping, or even seal launching, off. Don't try this at home.

Symonds Yat East is 500m past on river left; the landing steps are part of Wyedean Canoe Centre.

Symonds Yat rapid, author and dad! Photo | Lucy Perry.

Symonds Yat rapid.

Section 13

Symonds Yat East to Monmouth

Distance 8.4km
Start Symonds Yat East SO 561 160 / HR9 6BY
Finish Monmouth SO 512 129 / NP25 3SH
Difficulty Grade 1, one grade 2 rapid

Introduction

This short but glorious trip is one of the most popular in Britain. The Wye flows through a densely-wooded gorge, including of course the famous and (mildly) daunting Symonds Yat rapid, a place where many paddlers have enjoyed their earliest whitewater experience.

Launch points

Symonds Yat East SO 561 160 / HR9 6BY – the car park belongs to Wyedean Canoe Centre. Launch from the car park or at the upstream set of launching steps, beside the seal launch ramp.

Monmouth SO 512 129 / NP25 3SH – on river right just past the rowing club are a wide set of steps leading to a small parking area.

Nearby attractions

The gorge is surely attraction in itself; the Forestry England car park at Yat Rock is a

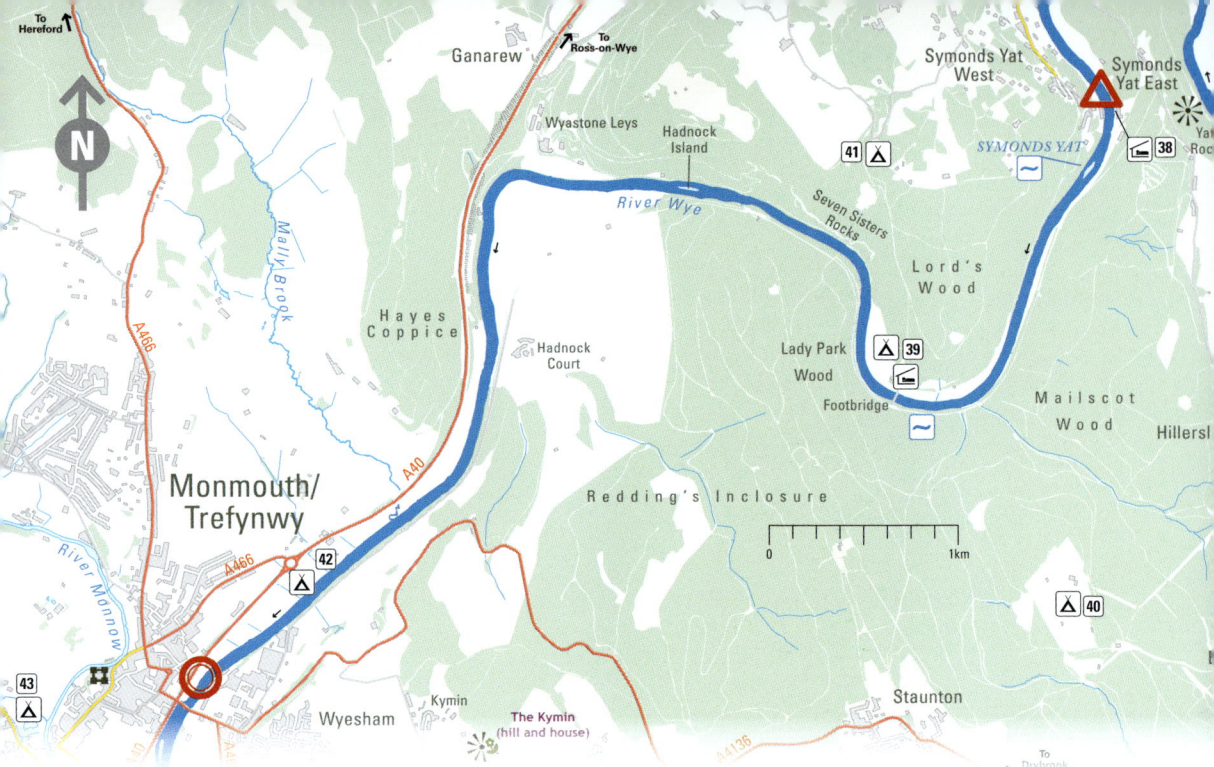

good start point for walks and cycles. The Peregrine Path cycle trail leads from Symonds Yat East to Monmouth, following the river along the former railway line.

The Forest of Dean sprawls to the south and east, offering no end of attractions and activities. A good start point is Beechenhurst Lodge, the Forestry England Visitor Centre, where there is an engaging 'Sculpture Trail'. Close by are the singletrack mountain bike trails of the Cannop Cycle Centre (start from the Pedalabikeaway shop).

Accommodation

The following campsites are beside the river: Biblins Youth Campsite (only available to family and youth groups, also has a bunkhouse), and Wye Tipi Camping. The following campsites are nearby: Bracelands Campsite, and Doward Park. B&B and hotel information can be obtained from Monmouth Tourist Information 01600 775257 and Wyedean Tourism.

Description

"A chasm between two ranges of hills which rise almost perpendicular from the water." (William Gilpin, *Observations on the River Wye* 1783)

Symonds Yat probably takes its name from Robert Symonds, a 17th-century Sheriff of Herefordshire. 'Yat' is ye olde slang for a gap or gateway between hills.

Launching from the steps of Wyedean Canoe Centre, right away you pass the hand-powered chain ferry which leads from the Saracen's Head Inn on river left. The author remembers visiting during family holidays as a boy, and marvelling at marks on the pub wall denoting the height of historical floods. These have long since been removed.

Within sight of the Saracen's Head is the horizon line of Symonds Yat rapids, where most of the current flows left of an island. It's possible, with care, to climb out on river left upstream of the rapids and inspect from the path running along the bank, but it is much easier to have done this beforehand, walking down from the car park. The rapids and island are just downstream of the site of New Weir Ironworks, and they are partly formed by traces of the weir and slag waste. In the main river left channel, the current has been funnelled and accelerated by a series of artificial groynes. Paddling straight through, there is little to concern the paddler other than a few waves splashing over your bows, and a slight bend to the right. However, the groynes mean that you can stop and learn or practise basic whitewater skills; this is an excellent place for breaking in, breaking out, ferry gliding and surfing waves. There are even small stoppers to side-surf at some higher water levels. The water is shallow so remind any swimmers to keep their feet up! At the end of the 150m-long rapids, there is a set of steps on river left for those who wish to return to the car park, or perhaps carry up and go again.

Right of the island is much less interesting, but be alert for low hanging tree branches. The water is often very shallow here, and paddlers sometimes wade upstream dragging their boats.

Symonds Yat rapids have been owned by Canoe England since 2009, when £250,000 was raised from sources such as the National Lottery. Although there is of course an unquestionable right of access to the rapids regardless of who owns them, CE ownership allows for them to be developed as a training site; for instance, there had previously been talk of removing the groynes and deepening the riverbed to make it more suitable for fishing.

The waters ease downstream of the rapids, allowing you to appreciate the thick woodland enveloping both banks. High above, limestone crags stand proudly clear of the tree canopy; the surrounding hills are as close here as at any point in the Wye's long journey. After a

Symonds Yat East chain ferry.

kilometre, the river left bank is known as 'The Slaughter', possibly because deer coming to the water to drink were shot here, but also reputedly because this was the site of an epic (mythical) battle between Romans and Ancient Britons. Here, the slopes fall back slightly on river right; this meadow is Biblin's Youth Campsite. You can't use their landing stage unless you are staying there, but if you do find yourself ashore, go look for the Dropping Wells (SO 551 145), 100m inland from the Wye. Here, a stream emerges from the crag behind the campsite and falls to the valley floor, forming overhanging tufa deposits. Tufa is a rare and beautiful limestone formation, created by calcium carbonate deposited over thousands of years.

A long, bouncy rapid leads past the campsite to a metal 'swinging' footbridge which has been here since 1957, with occasional renovations and a substantial rebuild after Storm Dennis's floods in 2020. On river left below is Lady Park Wood, a National Nature Reserve run by Forestry England. If the woodland seems even denser here than before, it is because it has been left alone without interference or management since the 1940s. This is a nationally important site for understanding woodland ecology.

When the Wye bends left, a series of crags become visible above the trees on river right. These are the Seven Sisters Rocks, although it is debatable how many of them there actually are. Hidden in the trees around them

Below Symonds Yat rapid.

are numerous quarry sites, and historically the limestone was brought down to the water to be shipped downriver. Above the crags is King Arthur's Cave, where prehistoric remains have been found. Opposite on river left is Far Hearkening Rock, so-named as gamekeepers listened for poachers from this lofty perch. The lovely, almost still, stretch of river below these high points is Martin's Pool, reputedly 20m deep.

A kilometre from the right bend, the river mostly flows left of Hadnock Island, originally formed by rocks fallen from above. This is the end of the gorge, as the river left bank opens out. The river right bank however still rises 200m above the river; the hill of Little Doward is topped by an Iron Age hill fort, which was cleared of trees in 2008. Down at river level, below this Woodland Trust reserve, are the remains of a limekiln. The houses you see just past this are Wyastone Leys. This estate dates from 1795 and was developed in the 1830s by Richard

Monmouth.

King Arthur's Cave

In the 19th century, this cave was home to Slippery Jim, a fur trapper who boasted of going 30 years without washing. In the 18th century, it is believed to have sheltered a locally notorious coracle salmon poacher, Tom O'Neill. These men were far from the first residents, however; the Reverend W S Symond excavated the cave in 1870–71, finding human remains from 12,000 years ago, alongside bones of mammoth, woolly rhinoceros and sabre toothed tigers. This location was near the southern limit of the ice sheet during the last Ice Age. Symond destructively used explosives to cut down through the layers of deposits, however in the 1920s, similar finds were made and investigated more scientifically at Merlin's Cave near Old Forge. Today, King Arthur's Cave is home to endangered lesser and greater horseshoe bats.

New Weir

The Symonds Yat rapids and island were the site of New Weir Forge ironworks, established around the 1570s. A sizeable weir was built in the 17th century, leading from the river left bank diagonally downstream to the site of the current island, where water was diverted to power the ironworks' waterwheels. This was of course an obstacle to river trade. Boats had to be dragged upstream by horses or humans through a sluice lock located along the river left bank, an awkward and dangerous process. The weir was removed in 1814. The Wye Tourists were not dismayed by this industrial scene. Conversely, it was regarded as a Tour highlight ...
"The violence of the stream, and the roaring of the waters impressed a new character on the scene: all was agitation and uproar, and every steep and every rock stared with wildness and terror."
(William Gilpin, *Observations on the River Wye* 1783)

Blakemore who constructed a deer park on the Little Doward; the fallow deer you might see today are probably descendants. Wyastone Leys now belongs to Nimbus Records who have a recording studio and concert hall here.

Between the Biblins and Wyastone Leys, the Wye has been the Anglo-Welsh border. Now it bends left and leaves England (until Redbrook, section 14), and henceforth is (almost) always heading south to join the River Severn. The 3km into Monmouth are unfortunately always within earshot of the A40, but at least it is out of view. Rowers frequent this stretch, so be alert. At Dixton, 12th-century St Peter's Church is passed on river right, with steps where the vicar used to take a ferry across to his vicarage. A series of flood height markers at the church entrance are daunting; one marked '1606' is at head height! This refers to the surge of 20th January 1607 (the marker is based on the old calendar), Britain's greatest natural disaster. Eye witnesses recorded, *"huge and mighty hills of water, tumbling over one another, coming with swiftness"*. Over two thousand people drowned in what was probably a tsunami triggered by an earthquake.

A kilometre below is Monmouth Bridge. The take-out steps are just upstream, after the steps leading to the huge rowing club building.

📷 Symonds Yat rapid.

Approaching Bigsweir Bridge.

Downstream of Monmouth.

Section 14

Monmouth to Brockweir

Distance 15.2km
Start Monmouth SO 512 129 / NP25 3SH
Finish Brockweir SO 539 012 / NP16 7NG
Difficulty Grade 1, one or two rapids perhaps reach grade 2. Tidal water towards the end.

Introduction

This section deserves to be much more popular with paddlers. Below Monmouth, the Wye flows determinedly south with many rapids; its current hemmed in and quickened by close valley sides. You pass through an attractive wooded vale, which permits occasional glimpses as to the industrial heartland this once was. The finish is on tidal waters.

Launch points

Monmouth SO 512 129 / NP25 3SH – the launching area is hard to locate, being accessed by a tunnel leading off Old Dixton Road under the A40 to the rowing club. Launch on river right using the downstream of the two sets of steps here. There is plenty of parking.

Brockweir SO 539 012 / NP16 7NG – land on river left, just upstream of Brockweir Bridge. The old stone quay is usually caked with tidal mud and unappealing; you are better off choosing the least muddy patch of bank, further upstream. There is parking for a handful of vehicles. Ideally arrive within two hours of local high water, which is around four hours before HW Dover.

Nearby attractions

There is of course plenty to do and see in Monmouth, see boxed text. Above the town, The Kymin offers fine views and a pleasant picnic spot. To the east, St Briavels Castle survives as an impressive gatehouse, also in current use as a youth hostel.

The Kymin Round Tower, Monmouth.

Accommodation

There are no campsites close by, see the following section for ideas. YHA St Briavels Castle is some distance east. B&B and hotel information can be obtained from Wyedean Tourism, 01594 810000 and Visit Monmouthshire.

Description

Launching from the steps upstream of Monmouth Bridge, note the wooded hill opposite, topped by a white tower; this is The Kymin (see boxed text). Monmouth has been a port since Roman times. The warehouses that once lined the banks were demolished in the 1960s to make space for the A40; now only one of the old quays remains, restored in 2009. Parts of Wye Bridge date from the 17th century. Just below is the first rapid of the day, which leads down to the river left side of an island. The River Monnow then joins from river right; this sizeable tributary is actually easy to miss, unless it is flowing well after rain. Two former railway bridges follow in close succession. The first dates from 1874 and is a girder bridge with three spans. The second dates from 1861 but was partly demolished after the closure of the line in 1964. The span across the river is gone, but the adjoining viaduct on river right is still intact, with 20 spans leading to nowhere! Debris from the demolition has formed a rocky rapid below; in low water some manoeuvring may be required to find a clear passage down. The confluence of the small River Trothy is inconspicuous on river right, and then the valley sides close in. Henceforth until Chepstow, the Wye is enclosed by a wooded gorge of Lower Devonian Sandstone. These are some of the most diverse woodlands in Britain, including beech, hazel, lime, pedunculate oak and

The Kymin

The hill overlooking Monmouth from the opposite (river left) bank of the Wye is The Kymin. The hill's summit is topped by a white roundhouse which stands alongside a temple commemorating Britain's naval victories. Ten counties can supposedly be seen from this viewpoint. The buildings and the park around are owned by the National Trust. Admiral Nelson himself visited the temple in 1802, his arrival honoured by cannon fire from the summit. He was accompanied by his mistress Lady Emma Hamilton, and fittingly some of his love letters to her are displayed in Monmouth's Nelson Museum. The great man inspected local woodlands for naval building potential and ordered more oaks to be planted. He also took a boat tour on the Wye, which failed to impress; he called it, *"such a little gut of a river"*.

sessile oak. In autumn, these form a glorious technicolor backdrop of green, brown, red, orange and yellow, well worth a visit.

After entering the woodlands, watch the river right shore carefully; for centuries the village of Penallt was a centre for producing 'puddingstones' (millstones) from locally-quarried quartz conglomerate. Amazingly, some of these still litter the banks.

When you see a black metal bridge crossing the river diagonally, you have reached Redbrook Bridge. Now a footbridge, from 1876 to 1959 this carried the Wye Valley Railway from England to Wales. From Monmouth you have been in Wales, for the remainder of its course, the Wye is the Anglo-Welsh border. Redbrook is on river left, but barely noticeable from water level. Redbrook's name comes from iron-ore stained streams which entered the Wye at this point. In 1880, a barge was robbed at Redbrook of its cargo by a mob, the only recorded act of piracy on the Wye!

A long rapid leads out of town where the A466 comes close. Several hundred metres on, huge boulders span the river creating another rapid. The rapids on this section are usually the remains of previous artificial weirs or other human activity. The construction of a weir hereabouts in the mid-16th century led to legal action after the price of fish in Monmouth doubled.

Whitebrook Stream which joins from river right was so named as it was polluted by the paper mills upstream, which were present from about 1760 into the 19th century, and produced bank notes. Prior to this, the stream

Monmouth

Monmouth's most famous landmark is on the town's other river; Monnow Bridge with its 13th-century gatehouse. Other attractions include the Nelson Museum, the 17th-century townhouse of Cornwall House and 11th-century Monmouth Castle, the birthplace of Henry V. The statue outside the Shire Hall is of local worthy Charles Stuart Rolls, co-founder of Rolls-Royce. His statue holds a model biplane, disappointingly alluding to his contribution to the development of aircraft engines, not to his other claim to fame; being the first Briton to die in a plane crash. In 1839, the Shire Hall hosted the trials of the Chartist leaders who had instigated a rising in South Wales. These advocates of greater parliamentary democracy were sentenced to death by hanging, drawing and quartering, but had their sentences commuted to transportation to Tasmania.

powered a branch of Tintern wireworks which was established here from 1606. Whitebrook is just a quiet back road today, unrecognisable as an industrial centre.

The graceful iron arch of Bigsweir Bridge was a toll bridge, built in 1828 to serve the new turnpike (toll road) opened along the valley in 1824. Prior to this, the only transport along the lower Wye valley was by boat! The parts for the bridge had to be brought upriver by

Bigsweir Bridge.

barge. Note the toll house on river right, which is now inhabited by protected bats. This is a significant spot as it is the Normal Tidal Limit (NTL) of the Wye. Henceforth the river is under the jurisdiction of Gloucester Harbour Trustees, not that you'll notice any difference. What you will notice are the muddy banks and silty brackish water. Henceforth, all rapids are dependent upon the tide; at high tide they vanish. William Coxe: *"The water is no longer transparent, and except at high tide the banks are covered with slime"*. (*An Historical Tour through Monmouthshire* 1801)

Between Bigsweir Bridge and the end of this section at Brockweir, Offa's Dyke Path follows the river left bank. About 600m downstream of Bigsweir Bridge is the site of the actual Bigs Weir, where the river widens into several channels around islands dividing up the water. Llandogo is seen ahead, on the outside of a left bend. High above this village in Cuckoo Wood is Cleddon Shoots Waterfall, where Wordsworth wrote the unimaginatively-titled poem 'Lines Composed a Few Miles above Tintern Abbey'. At spring high tides, Llandogo was the upstream limit for 50 ton trows (sailing barges) coming up from the Severn Estuary.

Ridingstream Weir is marked on the OS 1:25,000 map, but there is nothing of note here. However Coed-Ithel Weir 800m downstream has a distinct horizon line, and the water narrows forming a wavetrain over a very noticeable drop – of all the places on the lower Wye marked or named as weirs, this is the only one which is (almost) still a weir!

A final straight leads to Brockweir Bridge, a lattice girder construction from 1906. Approaching the bridge, search for a spot where you can disembark with minimal mud wading ... good luck with that!

Wintour's Leap.

Chepstow Castle.

Section 15

Brockweir to Chepstow

Distance 14.1km
Start Brockweir SO 539 012 / NP16 7NG
Finish Chepstow ST 537 942 / NP16 5HH
Difficulty Tidal water

Introduction

The Wye's final flourishes are truly spectacular, with soaring cliffs, beautiful woodlands and an engaging historical backdrop which spans millennia. This is however the most committing and challenging section of the Middle and Lower Wye, due to the powerful tidal flows and high mud banks.

Launch points

Brockweir SO 539 012 / NP16 7NG – launch on river left, just upstream of Brockweir Bridge. The old stone quay is usually caked with tidal mud and unappealing; you are better off choosing the least muddy patch of bank, further upstream. There is parking for a handful of vehicles.

Chepstow ST 537 942 / NP16 5HH – there is a floating pontoon across the road from the Boat Inn, belonging to Chepstow Boat Club. A donation is invited from users. The floating pontoon floats for (at most) two hours either side of local high water, which is around four hours before HW Dover. At other times, there is no option but to negotiate the deeply unpleasant and potentially dangerous mud banks.

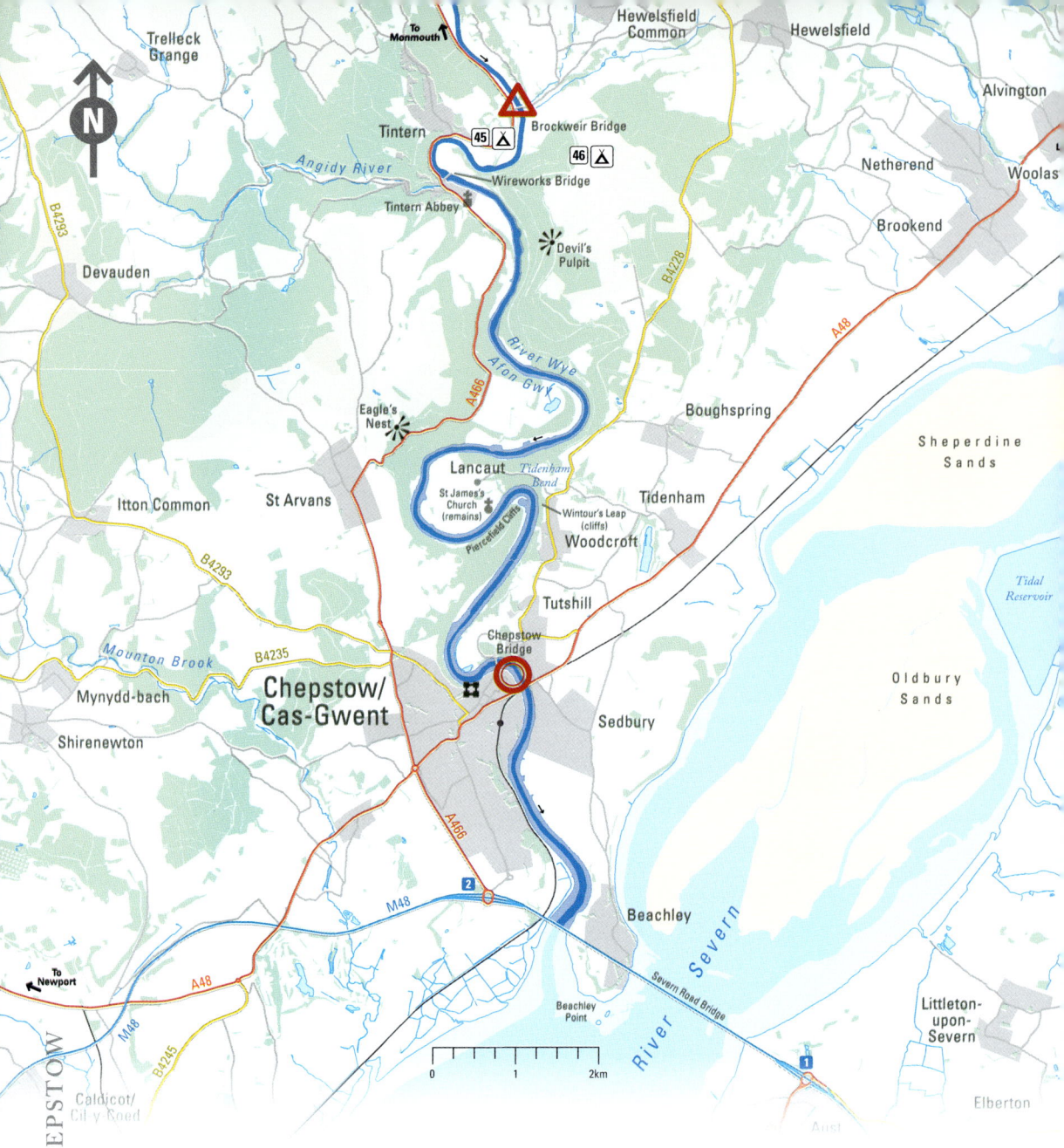

Nearby attractions

The highlight is of course Tintern Abbey, outlined opposite, but also find time to explore the neighbouring Angidy Valley, a birthplace of our Industrial Revolution. The Old Station near Tintern has a great tea room, plus displays and sculptures too. Walkers will have to choose between the viewpoints of Piercefield Park (river right) and those of the Offa's Dyke Path (river left).

Accommodation

The only potential camping beside the river is at Tintern Old Station, 01291 689566. Beeches Farm is high above Tintern. B&B and hotel information can be obtained from Chepstow Tourist Information Centre 01291 623772, Visit Monmouthshire and Wyedean Tourism, 01594 810000.

Description

This trip is unlike any upstream, as the Wye's flow is almost totally dictated by tides and as the tide falls, high banks of sucking mud are exposed, making getting out extremely difficult. Numerous weirs are named on the 1:25,000 Ordnance Survey map but these no longer exist, and you are unlikely to be paddling at the very low state of tide when any remains might affect the river's flow.

Brockweir is little more than a hamlet, its only amenity being an eco-shop. In the 19th century however, it was a sizeable port and ship-building centre, boasting 16 pubs! It seems to have been the 'Wild West' of the Wye Valley, known for drunkenness, fighting, gambling and prostitution. One visitor described it as: *"a city of refuge for persons of desperate and lawless character"*. The only trace of Brockweir's nefarious past is the preserved remains of Brockweir Quay, which is often obscured by mud.

Brockweir Bridge was built around 1907. Ferryman Edward Dibden took the bridge builders to the High Court in an attempt to stop con-

Tintern Abbey

Tintern Abbey originated in 1131, serving the Cistercian Order. Its current form mostly dates from the 13th century, although its ruined state is of course a consequence of the Dissolution of the Monasteries by Henry VIII in 1536. Draped in greenery and strewn with rubble, the abbey was a highlight of the Wye Tour. It was visited and immortalised in paint and prose by countless artists, most notably Turner and Wordsworth. The ruins seem to have been something akin to a theme park experience; rickety ladders and walkways allowed a thrilling exploration of the tops of the walls, while all around were makeshift huts touting tours, ferries to visit the Devil's Pulpit, and guided moonlight walks.

Today, the abbey grounds are administered by CADW. An entrance fee is payable, although much can be seen from a walk around the outside.

Tintern Abbey.

Brockweir.

struction and hence preserve his livelihood. The poor fellow lost and was bankrupted. If the tide is low, the river flows powerfully beneath the bridge, with a rapid to contend with. Just downstream on river left is a church, built in 1832 by Moravians who'd fled persecution to Britain. These Moravians moved from Bristol to preach to the sinful folk of Brockweir, building their church over a cockfighting pit.

The river describes the first of several large loops as it passes Tintern. On river right at the site of a former railway bridge and Lyn Weir is The Old Railway Station. The station hosts a tea room and railway carriages host the Destination Wye Valley exhibition, additionally there are sculptures, stalls and a small campsite. Landing might not be convenient if you are chasing the tide, nevertheless this is a pleasant visit when you get the chance. Further round the loop on river right, the Tintern Parva vineyard is seen, a restored version of the Tintern Abbey's vinery. Swift current and riffles are the only trace of Ash Weir, then you pass beneath Wireworks Bridge and the Angidy River joins on the right. This footbridge was built in 1876 to connect Tintern wireworks with the railway on the far bank but proved unnecessary as the works soon closed. A tramway joined the Wye at the mouth of the Angidy, today there are traces of a tidal dock from 1693, where there was also a tidal waterwheel. The dock has since been filled in for flood prevention.

Tintern Abbey is just below on river right, an impressive sight despite 500 years of decay. Landing is possible with care; a slippery bank can be scrambled up. If planning to visit the Abbey (and surrounding tea rooms?), factor time for this into your tidal scheming and take a long rope to secure your boat.

Leaving Tintern, scan the cliffs above on river left about 800m downstream. Offa's Dyke follows the top of these limestone cliffs, but you are looking for the Devil's Pulpit, a jutting crag which was a popular viewpoint of the Wye Tour. Supposedly the Devil tempted the monks from this lofty perch. These cliffs are the start of the Wye's 'lower gorge' of limestone cliffs, the first having been around Symonds Yat.

A kilometre past Tintern, the crag on river right is the Black Cliff, above the site of an ancient landslide. A further kilometre on the Ban-y-gor Rocks hove into view on river left, a line of vertical cliffs which have been somewhat sullied by quarrying. Look out for the Great Well where a stream of fresh water emerges from the tidal mud, forming a miniature bay. This is actually a 'resurgence', where water has sunk into the plateau above and passed through limestone caves. Many more can be seen before Chepstow, although some surface beneath water level. One such is Otter Hole, which stretches 3.4km from Alcove Wood under Chepstow Race Course, forming one of the longest and most pristine cave systems in Britain.

After passing Ban-y-gor Wood on river left, the Wye contorts into a 3km loop around the Lancaut peninsula before passing only 300m away from its start point. This dramatic loop passes below the Wyndcliff and Piercefield Cliffs on river right, popular viewpoints of the Wye Tour. At Martridge Wood, Tourists disembarked to climb the Wyndcliff. The Piercefield Cliffs extend down into the water towards the end of the loop. The remains of St

Piercefield Park

A visit to Piercefield Park was an essential part of the Wye Tour. In 1743, West Indies plantation owner Valentine Morris 'improved' the cliff top path by adding statues and viewpoints; the Alcove, Platform, Grotto, Giant's Cave, Lover's Leap, and Eagles Nest. Having blown all of his wealth on this project, Morris hurriedly left Britain to take up the post of Lieutenant-Governor of St Vincent. He returned from the West Indies after the French captured his island, finding that his wife had gone mad in his absence. He was imprisoned for his debts.

A later owner of the estate was Nathaniel Wells, who constructed the 365 steps leading up to the Eagles Nest viewpoint atop the Wyndcliff, 214m above the water. Wells was the son of slave and a plantation owner, and has the distinction of being Britain's first black High Sheriff.

The 2009 'Overlooking the Wye' project improved paths and cleared trees to revive some of Morris's viewpoints. The finest is undoubtedly the Eagle's Nest, where Coleridge rhapsodised about seeing, *"the whole world imaged in its vast circumference"*.

Journey's end, Chepstow.

James' Church are seen close by on river left, believed to be the site of an early Christian monastery, dating from 703. 'Lancaut' comes from *Llan* (church) and *Cewydd* (a Welsh saint). The present church was dedicated in the 1750s, but it fell into disuse around 1865.

The Wye next bends sharply right around Tidenham Bend, beneath the towering crags of Wintour's Leap on river left. Wintour's Leap rises 60–70m sheer from the woods, some of the tallest inland cliffs in England. They are named for Sir John Wintour, who during the Civil War supposedly rode off them and swam the river to escape pursuing Roundheads. On the inside of the bend is a large bay which is actually another resurgence, but was used into the 20th century for mooring trows loading stone from the quarries. The woods behind shield a heronry. The high points on both the inside and outside of Tidenham Bend are topped with Iron Age hill forts – Piercefield and Spital Meend. Surely, one of the most impressive places on a river with no shortage of impressive places! The next section is Longhope Reach where the Wye is straight as a die for a mile, reputedly the longest straight below Hereford. A left bend then reveals a final treat; the walls, buttresses, towers and keeps of Chepstow Castle extend for 250m along the cliffs of the river right bank. Just amazing.

Chepstow Bridge is an 1816 construction of cast iron, with an elegant central span of 34 metres. Directly below on river left is a limestone cliff marked with a Union Flag painting and a peculiar square hole; this is known as 'Gloucester Hole' as it's

Chepstow Castle

"Its walls seem a continuation of the rock, from which towers and battlements rise up ... What was grim and threatening in its day of power and pride, is now softened into beauty by time and decay." (Louisa May Twamley *An Autumn Ramble by the Wye* 1839)

This awe-inspiring edifice originates from 1067, built by William FitzOsbern, Earl of Hereford. Granted power over the region by William the Conqueror, Osbern was responsible for a chain of frontier castles reaching up the Wye beyond Hay. Chepstow was the first stone-built Norman castle in Britain, an indication of how important this port and river crossing was. The castle was augmented and extended until 1690, but the multiple keeps and courtyards stretching along the cliffs actually make little defensive sense; more likely the main aim was to impress visitors. The castle was under siege during the Civil War in 1645 and 1648. Later it was used to imprison Sir Henry Marten, one of the regicides who signed Charles I's death warrant. He stayed in comparative comfort in 'Marten's Tower' from 1668–80.

in Gloucestershire, and is believed to be a natural cave which was enlarged for storage. Your take-out is directly opposite, on the river right bank ... hopefully the tide hasn't dropped so far as to make the pontoon inaccessible!

Chepstow.

Severn Road Bridge.

Chapel Rock at low tide.

Mouth of the Wye

The Mouth of the Wye

Distance	10km out and back trip
Start	Chepstow ST 537 942 / NP16 5HH
Finish	Chepstow ST 537 942 / NP16 5HH
Difficulty	Exposed and extremely powerful tidal water

Introduction

The short final reach of the Wye into the Severn Estuary is bleak and windswept, with little to reward the visitor beyond the solitude of open spaces. The few paddlers who venture out to the mouth of the Wye will need to be well equipped (sea kayaks recommended) and fully understanding of this extremely dangerous tidal environment. For these reasons it is frankly hard to recommend, but is described here for completeness.

Launch points

Chepstow ST 537 942 / NP16 5HH – there is a floating pontoon across the road from the Boat Inn, belonging to Chepstow Boat Club; a donation is invited from users. The floating pontoon floats for (at most) two hours either side of local high water, which is around four hours before HW Dover. At other times, there is no option but to negotiate the deeply unpleasant and potentially dangerous mud banks.

Nearby attractions

Chepstow Castle cannot be missed; as castles go, it's a particularly good one! Other attractions include the remains of the Port Walls and Chepstow Museum. Even if you never intend to paddle this challenging final section of the Wye, a drive and walk down to Beachley Point is recommended; perhaps at sunset, when the wading birds leave the mud to fly to their nests, and the lights of the Severn Bridge come to life.

Accommodation

No campsites here! B&B and hotel information can be obtained from Chepstow Tourist Information Centre 01291 623772.

Description

"[The] mouth of the Wye, where we found the tide uncommonly rapid, and where if the wind is brisk, the waters are troublesomely rough". (Samuel Ireland *Picturesque Views on the River Wye* 1797)

A visit to the mouth of the Wye is best achieved through a round trip, out and back

Severn Road Bridge.

from Chepstow. The safest approach might be to time your return to Chepstow at local high water. This would of course involve paddling against the incoming tide on the outward leg, so a neap (weaker) tide is preferable. Avoid this trip when the Wye is high, as this could hinder the upstream return.

Chepstow's name comes from Old English: *chepe* (market) and *stow* (town). It was the largest port in South Wales until the early 19th century, with three shipyards. Heavy industries grew elsewhere along the Severn estuary, leaving Chepstow dependent on its River Wye trade. The area around the Boat Inn where you launch was once known as 'The Devil's Half Acre' due to prostitution, but is now rather gentrified, with upmarket housing developments. From 1822, a popular daily steamer ship left this quayside for Bristol. Trade was reduced when the railway network linked to South Wales, at first via ferry, and eventually directly through the Severn Tunnel. The steamer packets remained in service until the First World War.

Directly downstream are two adjoining bridges; the modern A48 bridge and the tubular frame of the 1852 railway bridge. Both are high above the water to allow shipping to pass.

Samuel Ireland described how, *"The lofty and high impending screen of rocks, on either side of the river, rendered our passage downstream delightful"*. The cliffs are still present, on the river left and then the river right bank, but now topped by housing. Opposite the first cliffs on river right is the site of the former port of Chepstow, which became

National Shipyard No. 1 during the First World War. The cliffs downstream on river right are adjoined by the railway and topped by the houses of Bulwark, momentarily interrupted by a small Iron Age fort.

The M48 bridge is passed beneath alongside an army barracks on river left. Power cables held aloft by vast pylons cross the river high above. Then, the banks fall back, rimmed by mud banks and wide salt marshes … you have reached the Severn and the view to the left is dominated by the Severn Road Bridge. This is the narrowest part of the Severn Estuary; before the Severn Bridge was opened in 1966, Aust to Beachley was the route of a rather precarious car ferry. Going much further back, legend has it that Celtic bishops crossed here to meet St Augustine (representing the Roman church) in 603.

The currents here where the two rivers mingle are powerful, as can easily be seen while driving across the Severn Bridge; flows below reach 8–10 knots! Before turning back to Chepstow, judge how safe conditions are for a 200m paddle out to Chapel Rock (ST 548 900), surrounded by the Severn's flow. Also known as St Tecla's Island, this hillock of an island contains a navigational beacon (there has been some kind of light here since at least 1291) and the remains of St Twrog's Chapel. St Twrog supposedly lived here as a hermit, until murdered by Vikings. Her name has morphed

Pylon carrying cables across the estuary.

The National Shipyards

During the First World War, Chepstow and Beachley became home to the National Shipyards. These were created in 1917, after heavy U-boat losses, to rapidly construct prefabricated merchant ships. This was a vast enterprise; National Shipyard No. 1 was on the site of Chepstow's port and had eight separate slipways for launching ships. No. 2 was downstream at Beachley, on the site of the present Army base, and No. 3 was across the Severn at Portbury. However, no prefab ships were actually launched before the war ended and the scheme was criticised as a huge waste of resources.

over the centuries, variations including Twrog, Tecla or Treacle. Landing would be a precarious affair as the island is surrounded by mud-caked reefs at anything other than high tide. It is possible to trudge through the mud across from the shore at low tide, but this is obviously very dangerous and has sadly claimed lives in recent years.

Note that there is a potential evacuation point 800m to the north-east, just upstream of the Severn Bridge; Beachley Landing Pier (ST 552 907 / NP16 7HH) is one of the few all-tide launch points on the Severn Estuary, but it juts directly into the tidal flow and is also used by the Severn Area Rescue Association (SARA) to launch their lifeboat. Only make use of this spot if you are absolutely sure of what you are doing. Most will choose to turn around and paddle 5km back up to Chepstow, hopefully arriving back beside the Boat Inn around high tide.

Enjoying a trip down the Lower Wye (Wintour's Leap).

Access

"A gentle form of recreation that briefly makes a few birds wary."

Professor George Peterken OBE, the leading expert on the Wye's natural environment, describes canoeing.

Middle Wye and Lower Wye

Between the bridge at Hay-on-Wye on the Middle Wye and Bigsweir Bridge on the Lower Wye, the River Wye is subject to an undisputed Public Right of Navigation (PRN). The Environment Agency is responsible for regulating navigation under the Wye and Lugg Navigation Act. On the tidal waters from Bigsweir Bridge to the River Severn estuary, there is still a PRN, regulated by the Gloucester Harbour Trustees. What this means, simply, is that you can paddle freely year-round, and that your basic right to enjoy your river heritage is legally enshrined. Note however, that this does not give you right of access to the riverbank (notwithstanding 'incidental use' as outlined in the Act) except for at accepted public sites. If you wish to land or launch at a site, or to camp or picnic, you must first have permission from the landowner.

Above Hay-on-Wye, the status of navigation is disputed. The stretch between Glasbury and Hay has, however, for several decades been one of the most popular stretches for boating and swimming.

Upper Wye

The right to enjoy your river heritage on the Wye upstream of Hay-on-Wye is disputed. However, this does not mean that doing so is illegal.

> *"Some individuals are keen to point out that 'The Law' states there is no public right of navigation on water in England and Wales. In fact there is no statute, overriding or apparent, which supports this assertion."*
> Waters of Wales, www.watersofwales.org

This long-term legal vacuum has unfortunately encouraged some landowners and angling bodies to attempt to restrict access, most notably through introducing 'agreements' which are unfortunately not agreements but actually restrictions. British Canoeing, Canoe England and Canoe Wales, the governing bodies for paddlesport, reject the use of such 'agreements', sometimes called 'Voluntary Access Arrangements':

> "Voluntary Access Arrangements have been promoted by the Welsh Government as a way of resolving conflicts of use. Unfortunately some landowners and angling bodies have seen this as an opportunity to enforce their views and conditions on other user groups. This has led to VAAs being used as a way of granting restricted access to canoeists on terms determined by landowners and angling groups. These terms ... often display a one-sided interpretation of the law, with that group reserving a unilateral right to withdraw or amend the arrangement. These arrangements have not therefore been either voluntary or by agreement. They have not moved the position forward in managing and developing the use of inland waterways in a sustainable way. The way they have been used / misused has also served to harden the positions that they were supposed to address."
>
> Canoe Wales statement to Welsh Government consultation, Sept 2015

Along the Upper Wye are large blue signs erected by an angling group. While these signs have been funded from the public purse, and display official-looking logos, their legal validity has been, and continues to be, questioned. These signs peculiarly assume jurisdiction over how and when you should enjoy your river heritage: *"The owners of the river have granted access to and permission to navigate"*, and contain legally invalid and nonsensical statements, such as: *" ... by using this access point you are agreeing to the full terms of the Access Agreement"*. Canoe Wales is not of course part of any 'agreement'. Disregard the signs and use your own discretion and common sense in deciding how best to enjoy your river heritage.

Further advice is available from the websites listed opposite.

> In the unlikely event that you are challenged while paddling the Upper Wye, be polite and respectful, but do not be dissuaded from enjoying your river heritage. Should you feel threatened, or if you find your path physically barred, report this to the police just as you would in any other part of life. Also, log any incidents with Canoe Wales, who have a form for such purposes on their website.

Responsibilities

Whichever part of the Wye you choose to enjoy, it should go without saying that your basic right to enjoy your river heritage – whether legally enshrined or not – comes with respon-

Wye angler.

sibilities; most importantly, to respect and preserve the river environment for its own sake, and for others to enjoy. The Wye Valley AONB's *Code of Conduct for Canoeists on the Wye* (reproduced in this book) is a good guide to appropriate behaviour on the river, as is *The Canoeing Code* available from Natural Resources Wales.

Further information

Canoe Wales:
www.canoewales.com
British Canoeing:
www.britishcanoeing.org.uk
Access to Welsh rivers:
www.watersofwales.org
Access to British rivers:
www.riveraccessforall.co.uk
Natural Resources Wales:
www.naturalresources.wales

Camping

One of the greatest pleasures of a journey on the River Wye is pulling ashore, unpacking a tent and camping for the night. This must be done at recognised campsites, as wild camping is not permitted. The good news is that there is a large choice of campsites spaced out along the banks of the Middle and Lower Wye, and that most are delightful places which allow you to relax beside the river in relative peace and quiet. The Upper Wye is more limited in options for camping, and it should also be noted that there aren't many camping options on the Lower Wye past Symonds Yat.

Below are details of campsites, bunkhouses and 'glamping' options along or near the Wye. A few allow open fires. Most are closed over the winter months. Details of campsites change more regularly than any other aspect of this guidebook's information, so you are recommended to call ahead and check what is available before setting off!

Upper Wye

Name	Number on map	Section(s)	Grid reference	Postcode	Beside river (river right or river left)
Glangwy Farm Camping	1	1	SN 890 800	SY18 6RS	Y, (RR
Mid Wales Bunkhouse, Tipi and Camping	2	2	SN 998 750	LD6 5LY	N
Wyeside Camping and Caravanning Club Site	3	2, 3	SN 967 685	LD6 5LB	Y (RL
Beili Neuadd Bunkhouse	4	2, 3	SN 994 698	LD6 5NS	N
Doliago Farm Campsite	5	3	SN 967 638	LD1 6NU	N
Oak Grove Retreats at Doldowlod Caravan Park	6	3	SN 979 634	LD1 6NN	Y (RL
River Cabin Camping	7	6	SO 112 414	LD2 3TQ	N

📷 *Byecross Farm campsite.*

Phone	Website	Notes
07890 083630	www.facebook.com/2campsite	
01597 870081	www.bunkhousemidwales.co.uk	Camping and Caravanning Club members.
01597 810183	www.campingandcaravanningclub.co.uk	In Rhayader.
01597 810211	www.beilineuadd.co.uk	Bunkhouse only.
07870 537179	www.doliago.com	Near Llanwrthwl, offers 'near wild' camping.
07977 784316	www.oakgroveretreats.co.uk	Limited camping spaces, also offers 'glamping'.
01497 842998	www.rivercabin.co.uk	Near Llanstephan Bridge. Close to river but inaccessible.

CAMPING

Middle Wye

Name	Number on map	Section(s)	Grid reference	Postcode	Beside ri (river rig or river l
Wye Valley Canoes	8	6, 7	SO 180 392	HR3 5NP	Y (RR)
Digeddi Wildlife Camping	9	7	SO 203 406	HR3 5PR	N
Ashbrook Caravans and Camping	10	7	SO 212 413	HR3 5PP	N
Baskerville Hall Hotel	11	7	SO 212 433	HR3 5LE	N
Raquety Farm	12	7	SO 224 428	HR35RS	Y (RL)
Radnor's End Campsite	13	7	SO 224 431	HR3 5RS	N
Black Mountain View	14	7	SO 225 449	HR3 5RX	N
Whitney Toll Bridge	15	7, 8	SO 259 475	HR3 6EW	Y (RL)
Lockster's Farm	16	7, 8	SO 269 473	HR3 6EH	Y (RL)
Oakfield Farm	17	8	SO 270 462	HR3 5HJ	Y (RR)
The Weston	18	8	SO 311 459	HR3 6DD	Y (RR)
Byecross Farm	19	8, 9	SO 376 426	HR2 9LJ	Y (RR)
Preston-on-Wye Campsite	20	8, 9	SO 383 427	HR2 9JU	Y (RR)
Hereford Rowing Club	21	9, 10	SO 506 395	HR4 0BE	Y (RL)
The Moon Inn	22	10	SO 572 374	HR1 4LW	N
Lucksall Caravan and Camping Park	23	10	SO 568 363	HR1 4LP	Y (RL)
Woodland Tipi and Yurts	24	10, 11	SO 542 308	HR2 6QD	N
Tresseck Farm	25	10, 11	SO 548 292	HR2 6QH	Y (RR)
Lower Ruxton Farm	26	10, 11	SO 549 292	HR1 4TX	Y (RL)
Martha's Meadow	27	11	SO 598 282	HR9 6QY	Y (RR)
Backney Bridge	28	11	SO 582 272	HR9 6RD	N

Phone	Website	Notes
1497 847213	www.wyevalleycanoes.co.uk	'Posh bunkhouse' at Glasbury.
7772 554861	www.digeddi.com	Near Glasbury. Close to river. 'Rough' camping available.
1497 820583	www.ashbrook-caravans.co.uk	Near Hay-on-Wye.
1497 820033	www.baskervillehall.co.uk	Near Clyro. Book in advance. 'Dorms' also available. Swimming pool included!
1497 821520	www.racquetyfarm.com	Near Hay-on-Wye. Glamping available. Fires allowed.
1497 820780	www.hay-on-wye.co.uk/radnorsend	500m from Hay Bridge on RL.
7971 842997	www.blackmountainview.co.uk	Near Clyro.
1497 831669	www.whitneybridge.co.uk	At Whitney Bridge! Fires allowed.
1497 831391	www.poundbandb.co.uk	Behind the Boat Inn at Whitney-on-Wye.
1497 831373	www.campingriverwye.co.uk	Just downstream of Locksters Pool. Fires allowed.
1981 500396		At Turner's Boat. No water or toilets. Prior arrangement with Mr Price only.
1981 500284	www.byecrosscampsite.co.uk	At Bycross. Fires allowed. Yurts available.
1981 500349	www.wyecamphere.com	At Preston-on-Wye. Fires allowed, bring own wood.
1432 273915	www.herefordrc.co.uk	In central Hereford.
1432 873067	www.moonatmordiford.com	In Mordiford, 500m up the River Lugg.
1432 870213	www.lucksallpark.co.uk	Downstream of Holme Lacy Bridge. Landing by prior arrangement only.
1432 840488	www.woodlandtipis.co.uk	Between Hoarwithy and Little Dewchurch. Glamping only.
1432 840235	www.tresseckcampsite.co.uk	At Hoarwithy. Fires allowed.
1432 840223		At Hoarwithy. Limited facilities, prior permission from Mr Jenkins.
1989 562717	www.marthasmeadow.co.uk	At Foy. Camping and Caravanning Club members.
1989 567950	www.campingandcaravanningclub.co.uk	At Backney. Camping and Caravanning Club members.

Lower Wye

Name	Number on map	Section(s)	Grid reference	Postcode	Beside (river right or river left)
Mad Dogs and Vintage Vans	29	11, 12	SO 600 267	HR9 7JE	N
Ross Rowing Club	30	11, 12	SO 596 245	HR9 7BU	Y (RL)
The White Lion Inn	31	11, 12	SO 589 242	HR9 6AQ	Y (RR)
Ragmans Farm	32	12	SO 605 178	GL17 9PA	N
The Colliers Inn	33	12	SO 603 156	GL17 9PP	N
YHA Wye Valley	34	12	SO 591 177	HR9 6JJ	Y (RR)
Huntsham Bridge Camping	35	12	SO 568 181	HR9 6JN	Y, (RL)
River Wye Camping	36	12, 13	SO 556 174	HR9 6BY	Y (RR)
Sterrett's Caravan Park	37	12, 13	SO 556 172	HR9 6BY	Y (RR)
Ye Old Ferrie Inn	38	12, 13	SO 561 159	HR9 6BL	Y (RL)
Biblins Youth Campsite	39	13	SO 552 144	HR9 6DX	Y (RR)
Bracelands Campsite	40	13	SO 559 131	GL16 7NP	N
Doward Park Campsite	41	13	SO 548 157	HR9 6BP	N
Wye Tipi Camping	42	13, 14	SO 517 133	NP25 3SY	Y, (RR)
Monnow Bridge Caravan Site	43	13, 14	SO 504 126	NP25 5AD	N
YHA St Briavels Castle	44	14	SO 558 046	GL15 6RG	N
Tintern Old Station	45	14, 15	SO 536 006	NP16 7NX	Y (RR)
Beeches Farm	46	15	SO 547 006	NP16 7JR	N

Phone	Website	Notes
07854 499188	www.maddogsandvintagevans.co.uk	At Brampton Abbotts. 'Boutique glamping' only.
	www.rossrowingclub.co.uk	In Ross-on-Wye.
01989 562785	www.whitelionross.co.uk	Below Wilton Bridge.
01594 860244	www.ragmans.co.uk	Between Wye and Ruardean. Bunkhouse and yurt glamping only.
01594 860068	www.thecolliersinn.com	At Lydbrook. Bunkhouse only.
0845 3719666	www.yha.org.uk	At Welsh Bicknor. Camping available outside youth hostel.
07947 473795	www.huntshambridgecamping.com	Below Huntsham Bridge.
01600 890672	www.riverwyecamping.com	At Symonds Yat West.
01600 890886	www.sterrettscaravanpark.com	At Symonds Yat West.
01600 890232	www.yeoldferrieinn.com	At Symonds Yat West. Bunkhouse only.
01600 890850	www.biblins.org.uk	Downstream of Symonds Yat West. Only available to family and youth groups, book ahead. Bunkhouse available.
01594 837258 024 77986991	www.campingintheforest.co.uk	Near Berry Hill.
01600 890438	www.dowardpark.co.uk	Above Seven Sisters Rocks.
07885 759178	www.wyetipicamping.co.uk	In Monmouth. Fixed tipis and bell tents for hire.
01600 714004		In Monmouth. 1km up River Monnow.
0845 3719042	www.yha.org.uk	At St Briavels. Youth hostel only. It really is a castle!
01291 689566	www.visitmonmouthshire.com/oldstationtintern	At Tintern. Not always available. Difficult to access from river due to tides.
07791 540016	www.beechesfarmcampsite.co.uk	Located high above Tintern.

Swan and cygnets.

Wildlife and Environment

The flora and fauna of the Wye is something special, and paddlecraft might just be the best way to see and enjoy it!

A wide range of habitats and environments are encountered as the Wye progresses from the Cambrian Mountains, across the Herefordshire Plain, and down through limestone gorges to an estuarine environment. The river is relatively 'wild' having seen minimal alteration by human activity, and industry has now disappeared from the banks. The river is greener now than it has been for centuries. Hence, the Wye is home to a wonderfully diverse range of wildlife, but any change could potentially endanger this and appallingly, the river has seen significant ecological decline in just the five years since the first edition of this book was published..

Environmental issues

The Wye is unusual in being designated from source to mouth as both an SSSI (Site of Special Scientific Interest) and an European SAC (Special Area of Conservation). Seven of Britain's National Nature Reserves are found along the Wye.

The Wye Valley AONB

The river from Mordiford to Chepstow is the centrepiece of the Wye Valley AONB (Area of Outstanding Natural Beauty). This AONB covers 326 square kilometres of Gloucestershire, Herefordshire, Monmouthshire and the Forest of Dean, being the only one to straddle a national border. The AONB is unique in encompassing both river and forest environments (i.e. the River Wye and Forest of Dean). Just over a quarter of the AONB is woodland, of which 900 hectares are designated as an SSSI. Around 26,000 people live within the AONB, which is (understandably) a tourist hotspot; there are over 2.5 million visitor days recorded annually.

> "The Wye Valley Area of Outstanding Natural Beauty (AONB) is an internationally important protected landscape containing some of the most beautiful lowland scenery in Britain. Designated as AONB (the sister designation to National Parks) in 1971, the 92km stretch of the River Wye from just south of Hereford meanders through spectacular limestone gorge scenery and dense ravine woodlands to Chepstow. Superb wildlife, intriguing archaeological and industrial remains, and impressive geological features all make it into one of the most fascinating nationally-protected landscapes. The area has long been recognised as an exceptional landscape of national importance, attracting tourists for over 250 years. The Wye Valley AONB Partnership supports tourism and recreation, among other activities, that make a positive contribution to the conservation and enhancement of the outstanding natural beauty of the area."
>
> Andrew Blake, Wye Valley AONB Officer

Threats to the Wye

Undoubtedly, the greatest single threat to the Wye comes from industrial farming, especially that of chickens. The polluted run-off from vast quantities of chicken dung has measurably degraded the river in very recent times and this is currently a live issue that will determine the overall fate of the river. For further information, seek out the Guardian newspaper article *Shitstorm* reproduced at www.georgemonbiot.com, and also consider supporting the work of the campaign group River Action www.riveractionuk.com.

The Wye's ecosystem is also under threat from a number of invasive non-native species and diseases. On the banks, Himalayan balsam causes concern; this tall plant is spreading its range quickly and endangers the survival of native plants. From July to October, it is easily recognisable by its pink flowers.

Mink from the USA found their way into the river by the 1960s, and prospered due to the then absence of otters. By the 1990s, they had utterly exterminated the Wye's water voles. Although voles have been reintroduced and mink populations are now held at bay by the now-returned otters (which are far more aggressive than mink, but can't get into vole burrows), mink are still a scourge; the author has witnessed minks dragging freshly-killed voles.

Encroachments of signal crayfish from America in the 1980s brought crayfish plague, decimating white-clawed crayfish populations in the Lower Wye.

Gyrodactylus salaris (a salmon disease prevalent in Norway) and the *Dikerogammarus villosus* shrimp (from Eastern Europe, already present in British waters) are harmful waterborne species which have devastated fish and wildlife populations elsewhere. There is concern that paddlers could inadvertently introduce these to the river, through their boats and kit. If you paddle the Wye within seven days of paddling elsewhere, you should sterilise your equipment to reduce the risk of infecting the Wye.

Buttercup meadow.

Wildlife

There is so much to see and absorb, that proper justice cannot really be done to this here! Outlined below are some highlights of the River Wye's diverse flora and fauna.

Wild plants and flowers

In spring and early summer, look out for bluebells, wild garlic, chives and wood anemones along the banks, backed by meadows of wild flowers. Around 1,200 species of wild plants have been identified along the Lower Wye alone. The diversity of plant species generally increases along the river's length, as the Wye acquires more nutrients from tributaries and side streams. The agricultural Herefordshire Plain has the smallest plant diversity.

The plant life in the river itself is attractive too. Along the Upper Wye, look for the mosses and lichens on the rocky reefs channelling the rapids, and in the warmer months, the rushes which emerge from the water at quieter points. The Middle and Lower Wye are characterised by waving submerged fronds of water crowfoot, peppered on the water's surface by hundreds of tiny white flowers. This beautiful plant grows thickly wherever there are shallows, often denoting the site of old fords or weirs. Another common water plant is water milfoil, which has thin feather-like leaves and small reddish flowers at its tip.

The Wye's tidal reaches see a dramatic change in plant species. Salt marsh species such as scurvy grass and sea aster thrive in the muddy alluvium, shaded incongruously by thick tree cover reaching right down to the high tide line.

◉ *Floating over water crowfoot. Photo | Simon Crabtree.*

Trees

The Wye is defined by its trees, which grow almost continuously along its length from the high woodlands of the Cambrian Mountains to the dense forests hemming in the Lower Wye. Within the Wye Valley AONB, 26% of the land is forested, about 8,440 hectares! The Lower Wye's forests are ancient, the valley sides having been continuously covered since the last Ice Age. All along the Wye's length, the waterside trees are mostly alders and willows. Further up the bank slopes, oak, rowan and ash predominate. Autumn is a special time to paddle the Wye; the river becomes a long corridor of red, gold and orange.

Fish

The Wye drainage supports at least 29 different species of fish. Here can be found significant populations of: allis shad, Atlantic salmon, brook lamprey, brown trout, bullhead, carp, chub, dace, grayling, gudgeon, minnow, pike, river lamprey, roach, sea lamprey, stone loach and twaite shad. In the tidal parts, flounders and eels are also found.

Paddlers will be pleased to learn that they have no identifiable impact on fish (see Environment Agency Technical Report W266: The Effects of Canoeing on Fish Stocks and Angling) but even so, it is important when paddling in shallow spots not to disturb or dig up the gravel in the riverbed. *Wilfully* damaging redds is an offence.

Salmon

The river is famous amongst anglers for its salmon. These incredible fish migrate thousands of kilometres across the North Atlantic, before swimming all the way up the length of the Wye past Llangurig, where they lay their eggs in gravel spawning beds known as redds. Up to the early twentieth century, salmon netting was carried out on an industrial scale (this was the most netted river in England and Wales) on the Middle and Lower Wye. This inevitably led to the salmon population crashing, and in 1908 netting was outlawed above Bigsweir. The salmon populations subsequently recovered, only to crash again in recent decades. The reasons for this are likely to be connected to human factors such as climate change, Atlantic overfishing and agricultural pollution.

Mammals

More than 40 species of wild mammal frequent the shores of the Wye. Badgers, bats, brown hare, deer, foxes, hedgehogs, otters, rabbits and water voles are all commonly seen. Rarer sightings include stoats and weasels (one is weasily recognisable, while the other is stoatily different), and polecats and pine martens, which have both recently returned to the Wye. Wild boar and beaver were made extinct centuries ago, but the Lower Wye now boasts a well-established population of boar who escaped captivity!

Bats

Bats are a key reason for the Wye's SAC designation. There are 13 species in total, including Daubenton's bats and greater and lesser horseshoe bats. These small bats roost in caves, railway tunnels, mines and limestone quarries. The toll house at Bigsweir Bridge is one important habitat! Of course, you are unlikely to see bats while paddling but their insect-hunting swoops and low passes enrich any evening spent camping beside the river.

Deer

The Wye Valley AONB has a population of (at the very least) 1,200 deer. The most common are fallow and roe deer which have descended from escapees from deer parks. Red deer are the rarest, and there are also populations of muntjac deer. Hundreds are culled (i.e. shot) each year, but the population is growing and is now considered to be unsustainable, causing damage to the ecosystem. Deer can be encountered anywhere along the Wye. However, paddlers disciplined enough to be on the water early, and paddling quietly alongside areas where woodland descends to the water's edge (e.g. Capler Wood or Lady Park Wood), have a good chance of being rewarded with the sight of a herd emerging to drink.

Otters

Otters are back! Firstly hunting and then, more devastatingly, the use of organochlorine pesticides, wiped them out from the Wye below Hay-on-Wye by the end of the 1970s. These wonderful sleek predators have since recovered well and are now commonly seen along the whole river. While paddling, scan the banks for signs of their holts; these are underground resting places hidden beneath tree roots and foliage. Otters are territorial and return to these holts, although their 'home range' can span up to 40km of the

Fallow deer. Photo | istockphoto.com

Otter. Photo | istockphoto.com

river. Otters are most active nocturnally, with the best chance of watching them being at dusk or dawn; for example the author has experienced them swimming and hunting for fish in the very early hours, opposite a campsite not far downstream from Whitney-on-Wye. He has also encountered one sitting on a reef in mid-river on the Upper Wye in broad daylight, so those who hate early starts might still get lucky!

Insects

In summer, the air above the river's surface is alive – thick, even – with flying insects. Along the Upper Wye, mayflies and moth-like caddis flies breed, while further downstream the dragonflies and damselflies predominate – there are 28 species present. The most common is the club-tailed dragonfly, recognisable by its black and yellow body and iridescent wings. These lay their eggs on beds of water crowfoot. The erratic flying displays that you will witness are often territorial dogfights conducted above their eggs.

Birds

Where to start? A survey by the RSPB in 1977 identified 129 different bird species along the Wye, upstream of Monmouth. Bird lovers will never, ever tire of the Wye. Mute swans, herons, coots and ducks are a constant sight. Cormorants fish many stretches of the Wye, to the irritation of anglers. Outlined below are some of the Wye's 'star species'.

Kingfishers. Photo | istockphoto.com

Kingfishers

This iconic bird needs no introduction. The sudden, startling flash of turquoise blue and bright orange is a commonplace experience of paddling the Wye, but it never grows old. Less commonplace, is seeing a kingfisher make its incredibly sleek and precise dive to catch a fish; perhaps the key here is to wait and watch when a kingfisher has been located. A friend tried this patiently, taking numerous photos; checking the camera later, it emerged that she had been stalking a piece of brightly-coloured agricultural plastic.

Sand martins

Sand martins are present along the Wye (especially the Middle section) during the summer months, and lay on one of the river's finest spectacles. These small birds are dark brown on top, and light-coloured below, but regardless, you won't fail to recognise them. They live in holes burrowed out of the banks, the red-brown earth of eroded Old Red Sandstone seemingly being ideal for this. The burrows are often encountered in large clusters, and the martins constantly flit in and out of these, searching for and delivering insects for food. The effect is something like a sand martin city; paddlers find themselves paddling through mad flurries of birds, all gracefully and rapidly manoeuvring across the water and around each other at a breathtaking pace.

Wagtails and dippers

Grey wagtails, pied wagtails, yellow wagtails and dippers flit from rock to rock all along the Upper Wye. The dippers especially are an absolute delight, disappearing into the rapids in search of food along the riverbed, and emerging unruffled and unharmed. Wagtails and dippers are less common further downstream, where pesticides and agricultural discharge make the water murkier.

Peregrine falcons

These lightning-fast raptors nest in limestone cliffs high above the Lower Wye. If you are fortunate they can be spied as blue-grey blurs, streaking alongside the crags in pursuit of unfortunate prey ... a pursuit that rarely lasts long. Peregrines were virtually wiped out by the 1960s, due to illegal killing, egg collectors, and the impact of the pesticide DDT, which weakened their egg shells. The pair which bred at Coldwell Rocks beside Yat Rock in the 1970s was a cause for jubilation, and signified the start of national recovery. Peregrine nest locations are often guarded and kept secret, but they are now even found in the centre of Chepstow!

Red kites

Red kites wheel around dominating the skies above the Upper Wye, scanning the fields and mountainsides below for worms, insects, mammals or carrion. Their 170cm wingspan, forked tails and red-brown colouring are unmistakeable, and their screeching whistles send a chill down the spine. After human depredations during the 19th century, by the 1930s only two pairs survived in all of Britain. These were in Mid Wales and it is this now-recovered population which is almost always in view – often in huge numbers – along the Wye above and around Rhayader. The red kites which have become common in other regions were reintroduced; birds in the Wye population are the 'originals'!

A peregrine falcon nest – look closely!

Red kite.

Approaching Goodrich Castle.

Culture and Landscape: The Story of the Wye

The River Wye has been shaped by geological processes spanning millions of years, and by thousands of years of human activity. One of the pleasures of paddling the river is seeing this 'story' writ large in the landscape around you.

Geology

The geology of the River Wye is fairly simple to grasp; the further downstream you paddle, the younger rocks tend to become. This is of course counterintuitive, as you might expect the river to be cutting down into older strata.

The Upper Wye

The oldest rocks are found around the Wye's source atop Plynlimon Mountain, dating from the Ordovician Period (485–444 million years ago). These oceanic mudstones, shales and sandstones are more easily eroded than the older volcanic Ordovician rocks of the Snowdonia peaks to the north, hence Plynlimon's rounded profile. The mountains through which the Upper Wye slices southwards are younger but similarly rounded, being formed by more oceanic sandstones, siltstones and mudstones from the Silurian Period (444–419 Mya). These rocks are resistant enough to form a narrow valley and many bedrock rapids along the Upper Wye's course. The Wye cuts through a second band of Ordovician rocks between Llanwrthwl and Newbridge, although this makes no difference to the river's character. Silurian mountains again hem in the river south of Builth Wells, but around 4km south of Llyswen it reaches the Old Red Sandstone which heralds the end of the Upper Wye, and a dramatic change in character. The ocean that created the Ordovician and the Silurian Upper Wye geology has shrunk and closed; England and Wales finally collided with Scotland! The terrestrial geology of the Devonian awaits as you float onwards into the Middle Wye.

📷 *Penddol Rocks, a rapid formed by resistant Silurian geology.*

The Middle Wye

Although the river continues to flow upon Silurian sediments until near Fownhope, the character of the landscape to the south of the river is dominated by Devonian geology (419–359 Mya). These mountains, created by the collision of England and Wales into Scotland, are rapidly eroding (1cm in 50 years!). This provides coarse sediments that were transported by flash floods in an essentially arid Devonian Britain. The resulting Old Red Sandstone is a soft red-brown rock, formed from deposits of mud, sand and gravel; the distinctive red colour is iron oxide, more commonly known as rust. The Black Mountains and the hills past Hereford are formed from Old Red Sandstone. The exception is Woolhope Dome, an A-shaped anticline of folded Silurian sandstone, limestone and shales.

Due to the folded nature of the sediments, the oldest rocks are found in the centre of the hill. The fertile red-brown soils of the Herefordshire plain through which the Middle Wye meanders are formed from modern river alluvium eroded from the Black Mountains; this can easily be spotted in the red sandy banks of the river. The width of the flood plain corresponds to the local softness of Old Red Sandstone, hence the much wider plain approaching Ross-on-Wye. These sandstone soils are sometimes covered by successive terraces of gravel deposits laid down much later by meltwater in the Quaternary Period (2.6 Mya to the present), such as those around the River Lugg confluence, but the soil is always unmistakeable when exposed in eroded riverbanks.

The Lower Wye

The Old Red Sandstone is unmistakeable at Ross-on-Wye; the town is built atop an outcrop of it! A short distance downstream, Goodrich Castle almost appears to rear naturally from the stuff. However, the Lower Wye is characterised by very different geology. Although the Old Red Sandstone continues to underlay the landscape, it dips into a basin ('syncline') which is overlaid with limestone from the Carboniferous Period (359–299 Mya). The Old Red Sandstone continent eroded to such an extent that it was invaded by a warm, shallow sea. The limestone was formed by tropical carbonates and the remnants of organic creatures laid down upon the seabed. The Wye is contorted by this harder limestone into a series of sharp bends, making progress by incising deep gorges at Symonds Yat and above Chepstow. This limestone landscape includes formations such as caves, tufa dams, limestone pavement and sinkholes. The rock is riddled with water courses, some of which form 'resurgences' at the bottom of the gorges. The stream emerging at The Slaughter near Symonds Yat has passed through a 14km cave system, and the Otter Hole system near Chepstow has some of Britain's finest stalactites, protected by the fact that the stream emerges below the high tide mark! Outside the gorges, the Wye's Old Red Sandstone is often topped by Devonian Quartz Conglomerate (a coarse-grained sediment known locally as 'puddingstone') which causes the valley sides to be steeper. Large boulders encountered in the river are often puddingstones which have slid down from above.

Limestone cliffs at Wintour's Leap, Lower Wye.

Below Chepstow, the bedrock of the Severn Estuary is red desert sandstone from the Triassic Period (252–201 Mya), covered by deep deposits of Quaternary alluvium – mud.

The course of the Wye

There is controversy over how and when the Wye found its route to the sea. The traditional view is that it happened through 'entrenched meanders'. The Lower Wye was originally around 300m higher (the height of the surrounding hills), and progressively cut down through approximately the same course as now. The course altered slightly on occasion, for example the two valleys joining from river left at Redbrook were the course of a meander present when the Wye was 115m higher. A more recent hypothesis is that the Wye found its current course relatively late; instead, it originally flowed east from Hereford into the River Severn, while the final gorge of the Lower Wye was actually formed by the River Monnow. The theory suggests that the Wye was eventually diverted to its 'true' path south after being obstructed by an ice-dammed lake which covered the Herefordshire plain.

History

Prehistory

Human history along the Wye dates back at least 12,000 years to the end of the last Ice Age; the remains of Palaeolithic hunters have been found at locations such as King Arthur's Cave near Symonds Yat. At this point glacial ice sheets still covered the Upper Wye.

Chepstow Castle.

Mesolithic hunter-gatherers left few traces, and only a smattering of standing stones and tumuli survive from the Neolithic and then Bronze Age farmers who followed them. After 800BC Iron Age people certainly left their mark through the vast earthen hill forts atop the valley sides. These occur all along the river but are densest along the Lower Wye, where intriguingly, some face each other across the river (such as those at Piercefield and Spital Meend). The function of the Wye hill forts is unclear, but possibly they controlled river trade, or mark a boundary between the Silure and Dobunni tribes.

The hill forts fell into disuse following the arrival of the Romans after 43AD, who mined iron in the valley.

Tintern from the Devil's Pulpit, high on Offa's Dyke.

Offa's Dyke

The natural boundary formed by the Wye valley was utilised in the building of Offa's Dyke, constructed for Offa of Mercia (757–796) to guard the western borders of his kingdom. This earthwork stretched approximately along the modern Welsh/English border and is now the longest archaeological monument in Britain. Over 20 kilometres of the dyke survives intact between Hereford and Chepstow, and from Monmouth down it parallels the river.

Castles

Following the Norman Conquest in 1066, Norman barons stamped their mark on the Wye by constructing a chain of stone castles overlooking the river, guarding important settlements and crossings. Remains of these punctuate the Wye all the way from Rhayader and Builth Wells in the heart of Mid Wales, downstream to the sea where the largest and most spectacular of all the Wye castles is found at Chepstow. In the wake of Norman castle building, Cistercian monks founded their first Welsh abbey at Tintern in 1131.

The Industrial Revolution

The Lower Wye gorges were among the first places in Britain to be industrialised. Resources of timber, iron ore and coal were available close to the river, which offered both a transport artery and power supply. Brass and wire were produced at Tintern as early as the 1560s! Industries which followed included shipyards at Llandogo and Brockweir, paperworks at Whitebrook, and iron, tin and copper works at Lydbrook and Redbrook. Don't be deceived by the current idyllic woodlands and sleepy 'villages' of the Lower Wye; incredibly this was a heartland of Britain's Industrial Revolution with crowded mill towns, smoke-belching factories and banks denuded of trees for fuel, far into the 20th century.

Weirs and navigation

For centuries the Wye has seen tension between bargemen navigating the river to transport goods, and 'netsmen' who dammed the river with weirs to create fishing pools and traps.

Navigation rights on the Wye were first established by King Edward I in the 13th century, from Hay down; the river was known through the Middle Ages as the 'King's High Stream'. Centuries of legal disputes commenced, such as that in the 1330s when Henry of Lancaster complained about the two metre weir protecting Tintern Abbey's salmon stocks. Some of the weirs actually belonged to the Crown, so it's not surprising that the problem persisted beyond 1640, when a Hereford court ruled, *"Weirs on the Wye are a nuisance and hindrance to navigation".*

The Rivers Wye and Lugg Navigation Act of 1662 authorised Sir William Sandys to build locks on weirs along the river, to allow barges to pass. There is little evidence that much was completed and in 1695 another Act of Parliament ordered the removal of all weirs,

New Weir on the River Wye, by Edward Dayes 1800. Photo | Wikipedia Commons.

to improve navigation. The only surviving weir was New Weir (at Symonds Yat), which had a lock. Barges could now navigate the river without obstruction, but unfortunately the Wye was now often too shallow! Various schemes to address this problem made little progress; for example in 1763 engineer Isaac Taylor's plan for 22 locks up to Hereford (at a cost of £20,900) was not completed.

New Weir, the last artificial obstruction to navigation on the Wye, was removed in 1814, after the iron works had closed down. The rapids here are partly formed by remains of the weir, and indeed rapids and riffles along the Middle and Lower Wye often denote the former presence of weirs.

The Public Right of Navigation from Hay-on-Wye downstream continues to this day.

Trade and transport

Traces of Roman quays at Monmouth and as far upstream as The Weir (near Hereford) show that goods have been shipped up and down the Middle and Lower Wye for millennia. This trade continued into the 19th century, when constant barge traffic connected Hereford (and sometimes even Hay) with the sea. Goods such as timber, iron ore and coal were carried in flat-bottomed barges known as trows, powered by oars, sails and – when going upstream – humans hauling on ropes. Other craft on the river included gondolier-style tourist barges and also coracles for fishing, propelled by single paddles. Poet Samuel Rogers observed, *"The coracles go down the river two at a time, one on each side, drawing the net along to sweep the river."*

The Wye and Lugg Navigation Act of 1809 resulted in a riverside horse towpath being completed in 1811 along the barge route, but as human-hauled barges travelled toll-free, this brutal means of upstream propulsion remained common: *"In passing the various weirs, they are obliged to fall, with all their force, flat on the ground, which is done by the shout of 'yo ho!'"* (Charles Heath, *Monmouth* 1804)

In 1828, river traffic was diminished by the completion of the road between Monmouth and Chepstow. However, the opening of the Hereford, Ross and Gloucester Railway in 1855 almost instantly ended river trade to and from Hereford, with the Ross and Monmouth Railway (1873) and the Wye Valley Railway (1876), linking Monmouth to Chepstow, killing off what remained. Trows still carried stone downstream from the Lancaut quarries in the early 20th century, but the river was now only navigable on the tidal stretch up to Bigsweir. Paddlers today can thank the invention of the railway for the solitude that they enjoy.

Railway traces at Ballingham Bridge.

The Wye Tour

Remarkably, the Lower Wye was the site of Britain's first package tour – the Wye Tour. In 1745, the Reverend Dr John Egerton of Ross-on-Wye started taking his guests on boat trips down the Wye. This idea took off after 1783, when William Gilpin published Britain's first illustrated tourist guidebook, snappily titled *Observations on the River Wye and several Parts of South Wales etc., relative chiefly to Picturesque Beauty; made in the summer of the Year 1770*. Gilpin was not interested in enjoying sights, but in judging them, *"by the rules of picturesque beauty"*. This involved viewing selected viewpoints through a 12cm mirror, with your back to them. Gilpin gave specific (and eccentric) criteria for what was aesthetically permissible within the mirror's 'picturesque' image. He classified the first day of the Wye Tour from Ross to Monmouth as, *"Grand and Beautiful"*, and the second day from Monmouth to Chepstow as, *"Awful and Sublime"*.

The Wye Tour thrived because the Napoleonic Wars limited foreign travel. By 1808, eight covered gondoliers were in service. Each carried eight wealthy passengers and three crewmen, who had the unenviable task of dragging the boat back upstream after each tour. Following Gilpin, Wye guidebooks proliferated (over 20 by 1850), with some brave authors venturing into wild Mid Wales to explore the Upper Wye. Turner, Wordsworth, George Bernard Shaw, Nelson, Dickens and Elgar all floated or walked the Lower Wye.

The Wye Tour was almost forgotten after the First World War, with only Peter Gordon Lawrence's 1950s canoe camping trips (this became PGL Adventures) recalling the use of the river for leisure. Of course the Lower Wye valley is now once more a popular tourist destination, with the industry worth at least £100 million annually to the local economy.

Other Activities

Outlined here are ideas for other outdoor activities within the Wye valley and surrounding areas.

Paddlesports

The Wye may be the finest touring river hereabouts, but it isn't the only one. Its bigger tributaries all offer opportunities for trips of at least two days; the Rivers Ithon, Irfon, Lugg and Monnow. They offer more challenging conditions than the Wye, with rapids up to grade 2, changeable water levels and hazards such as artificial weirs. Most are unlikely to be paddleable without recent rainfall, although the River Lugg is usually viable outside the summer months. The Lugg from Presteigne Town Bridge is part of the Rivers Wye and Lugg Navigation, meaning that the same protected access rights exist as on the Wye from Hay-on-Wye.

After heavy rain, a few of the Upper Wye's tributaries offer challenging whitewater, for example there are some undammed rivers in the Elan catchment, the upper Irfon is a grade 4 classic and the Afon Edw is a good grade 3 run. There is more to explore in the Brecon Beacons National Park, a short distance south of the Middle Wye.

English Canoe Classics – Volume 2 South, Eddie Palmer, Pesda Press, 2013, ISBN 9781906095413

The Welsh Rivers, Chris Sladden, Chris Sladden Books, 2012, ISBN 9780951614730

www.ukriversguidebook.co.uk

Walking

A vast network of footpaths means that the walking possibilities are almost infinite! A number of waymarked trails follow the Wye, the daddy of them all being the Wye Valley Walk. This 218km trail leads from Chepstow Castle to the summit of Plynlimon and is signposted by a 'leaping salmon' logo. Offa's Dyke National Trail starts at Sedbury Cliffs near Chepstow, and follows the Lower Wye in the early parts of its 283km route. Also check out the Gloucestershire Way, Herefordshire Trail and Wysis Way which all connect the Wye to other regions.

Offa's Dyke Path, Tony Gowers, Aurum Press, 2014, ISBN 9781781310663

The Wye Valley Walk, Wye Valley Walk Partnership, Cicerone, 2011, ISBN 978185284 6251.

Mountain biking

There are great opportunities for off-road riding in the Cambrian Mountains around the Upper Wye. Many challenging bridleways can be linked up, and the Elan Trail is a splendid easy (downhill!) ride to Rhayader. *The Good Mountain Biking Guide* is the best guidebook for this area.

Along the Lower Wye, the Peregrine Path cycleway is an excellent and easy riverside trail, following the former railway from Monmouth to Goodrich. The best challenging riding is nearby in the Forest of Dean at Cannop Cycle Centre.

The Good Mountain Biking Guide: England & Wales, Active Maps Ltd, 2018, ISBN 9780955919107

Climbing

The limestone cliffs of the Lower Wye's gorges are a mecca for crag rats, being among England's tallest cliffs. The crags around

The Elan Trail.

Climbing at Wintour's Leap. Photo | Stuart Yendle.

Symonds Yat alone sprawl over several volumes of guidebooks! The Wye's second limestone gorge offers an endless choice of vertiginous routes at several hotspots: Ban-y-gor Cliffs, Wynd Cliff and Wintour's Leap, as well as the quarries around them. The Forest of Dean also has climbing possibilities on sandstone scarps and quarries. The Climber's Club records the routes and publish several guidebooks.

Lower Wye Valley, John Willson, Climber's Club, 2007, ISBN 9780901601797

The Sandstone Outcrops of the Forest of Dean, Martin Crocker, Climber's Club, 2006, ISBN 0901601780

Symonds Yat, John Willson, Climber's Club, 2010, ISBN 9780901601872

Wye Valley, John Willson, Climber's Club, 2012, ISBN 9780901601919

Wye Valley Sport, Gordon Jenkin, Great Western Rock, 2021, ISBN 9781800681361

Code of Conduct

The Wye Valley AONB has kindly given permission for these extracts to be reproduced from their information leaflet, *Code of Conduct for Canoeists on the Wye*. The advice is intended for the Wye within the AONB, but is of course common sense for the whole river. The full leaflet can be ordered via www.wyevalleyaonb.org.uk.

Care for wildlife

Some fish species are particularly sensitive to disturbance, especially during the spawning seasons. During winter salmon spawn in the upper reaches of the Wye. Between 1st of April and 31st July many coarse fish are breeding and twaite and allis shad use shallow gravel beds for egg laying. Please do not land on gravel beds during this period and at all other times try to:

- Avoid disturbing nesting birds along the river banks, particularly in spring time.
- Avoid damaging beds of waterweed.
- Stop your activity if you are clearly disturbing wildlife.
- The river habitat and many of the species it supports are protected by law. Ignoring this advice could result in a criminal offence being committed, and you may be subject to enforcement action.

Stay safe

- Use the river in a safe fashion and ensure that you have the appropriate safety equipment.
- Ensure that any groups of young novice boaters are led by suitably experienced responsible persons – preferably a qualified instructor.
- Don't drink alcohol during and just prior to your trip on the river.
- Follow instructions given to you by your canoe hire operator and/or group leader.

Help keep a healthy river

- Take your rubbish away with you.
- Avoid damage to banks, the riverbed and bankside vegetation – this can lead to erosion. You can help by only launching and landing at purpose-made launch points.
- Avoid dragging boats and equipment over rock slabs and stones.

Be fishing friendly
- Pass anglers with as little noise and disturbance as possible.
- Keep away from banks being fished and fishing tackle.
- Avoid loitering in pools if anyone is fishing.
- Comply with reasonable directional requests.

Consider other people
- Park sensibly without causing obstruction, do not block gateways or load and unload vehicles in awkward places.
- Keep noise to a minimum.
- Get changed out of public view.
- Whenever possible come ashore at recognised landing places; do not trespass on private property or moorings.
- When canoeing have special regard for beginners, as you would for learner drivers on the road.
- Remember that larger boats are less manoeuvrable and cannot use such shallow waters as canoes, rafts and rowing boats.
- Give way to those engaged in organised competition and have regard to any instructions given by officials.
- Hail to draw a person's attention to a situation which might otherwise result in inconvenience, damage or collision. Please treat a hail as a friendly warning and not as an insult.

Further Information

Tourist information

www.visitmidwales.co.uk – Mid Wales
www.visitherefordshire.co.uk – Herefordshire
www.wyevalleyaonb.org.uk – The Wye Valley AONB
www.visitdeanwye.co.uk – Lower Wye Valley and Forest of Dean
www.riveractionuk.com – River Action UK, anti-pollution campaign group

Useful books

The Archaeology and History of Ancient Dean and the Wye Valley, Bryan Walters, Thornhill, 1992, ISBN 0946328420

Herefordshire's River Trade, Heather Hurley, Logaston Press, 2013, ISBN 9781906663759

Landscapes of the Wye Tour, Susan Peterken, Logaston Press, 2008, ISBN 9781904396895

The Natural History of Wales, William M. Condry, Collins New Naturalist, 2009, ISBN 9780007308422

Overlooking the Wye, Ruth Waycott, Black Dwarf Publications, 2013, ISBN 9781903599211

River Voices, Marsha O'Mahony, Logaston Press, 2018, ISBN 9781910839317

Woodlands of the Lower Wye, George Peterken, Wye Valley AONB, 2007

The River Wye – A Pictorial History, Josephine Jeremiah, Phillimore & Co. Ltd, 2004, ISBN 186077301X

The Wye Tour and its Artists, Julian Mitchell, Logaston Press, 2010, ISBN 9781906663322

The Wye Valley, Edmund J. Mason, Robert Hale Limited, 1987, ISBN 0709029640

Wye, Richard Hayman, Logaston Press, 2016, ISBN 9781910839096

Wye Valley, George Peterken, Collins New Naturalist, 2008, ISBN 9780007160693

Historical sources

A journey down the Wye is arguably enhanced by knowing what earlier travellers experienced, and why they viewed the river in the way that they did. The following accounts are among those cited in this guidebook:

An Autumn Ramble by the Wye, Louisa Anne Twamley 1839

An Historical Tour through Monmouthshire, William Coxe 1801

Camping on the Wye, S. K. Baker 1892

Coming down the Wye, Robert Gibbings 1942

Observations on the River Wye and several Parts of South Wales etc., relative chiefly to Picturesque Beauty; made in the summer of the Year 1770, William Gilpin 1783

Picturesque Views on the River Wye, Samuel Ireland 1797

Scenery of the River Wye, Thomas Roscoe c. 1839

The book of South Wales, the Wye and the Coast, Mr and Mrs S.C. Hall 1861

The Wye: A Picturesque Ramble, Leigh Ritchie 1841

Topographical Dictionary of Wales, Sam Lewis 1833

Wanderings and Excursions in South Wales, Thomas Roscoe 1837

Wye Tour, Thomas Dudley Fosbroke 1822

Index

A

Aberedw Rocks 61, 63
access 143
activities 168
Angidy Valley 130
Apple Oak Day 95

B

bats 157
Beachley Landing Pier 141
Beachley Point 138
Beechenhurst Lodge 116
Bigsweir Bridge 126, 127
birds 158
Black Mountains 74, 76
Boatside Weir 76
Boughrood Bridge 67, 69
Bredwardine Bridge 79, 82
Brobury House 79, 82
Brobury Scar 82
Brockweir 123, 129, 131, 132
Brockweir Bridge 127, 129, 132
Bronllys Castle 67
Brynwern Bridge 59
Bryn-wern Hall 59
Builth Castle 63, 64
Builth Wells 57, 59, 61, 62, 64
buoyancy 19
buoyancy aid 20
Butterfly Zoo 108
Bycross 79, 85
Byecross Farm Campsite 79, 83, 85, 86
Byford 85, 87
Byford Church 85

C

camping 146
campsites 146, 148, 150
Cannop Cycle Centre 116, 169
canoe hire 17
canoes 15
Capler Camp 95
Carey Islands 95
Carn Gaffallt Bird Reserve 54
carrying gear 18
castles 165
caves 133, 163
Chapel Rock 140
Chepstow 129, 137, 139, 141
Chepstow Boat Club 129, 137
Chepstow Bridge 134
Chepstow Castle 134, 135, 138
Chepstow Museum 138
cider 86, 88
Clifford Castle 76
climate 12
climbing 169
clothing 20
Code of Conduct 170
Coed-Ithel Weir 127
crayfish 154

D

deer 157
Devil's Bridge 41
Devil's Pulpit 133
Dikerogammarus villosus 154
dipper 159
distances 13
Doldowlod House 55
Dolhelfa 45, 47, 48
Dropping Wells 118
Duke of Edinburgh's Award 27, 28, 30

E

Edw, River 168
Elan, River 53
Elan Trail 169
entrapment 19
Environment Agency 22
environmental issues 153
equipment 18
Erwood 61, 65, 67
expeditions 24, 26, 27

F

falcon 159
fish 156
flotation 19
flow 12
flowers 155
Forest of Dean 116
Fownhope 95

G

gear 18
geology 161, 162, 163

Gigrin Farm Red Kite Centre 52, 53
Gilfach Nature Reserve 46, 49
Glasbury 67, 69, 73, 75
Glasbury Scout Hut 75
Gloucester Hole 135
Goodrich Castle 108, 111
Gospel Pass 74
Great Flood of 1795 69
Gyrodactylus salaris 154

H

Hay Bridge 76
Hay Festival of Literature 77
Hay-on-Wye 73, 74, 77
hazards 19, 20
Hell Hole 68
help 22
Hereford 85, 88, 91
Hereford Castle 93, 94
Hereford Cathedral 85, 88, 89, 93
hill forts 164
hire, equipment 17
history 164
Hoarwithy 91, 96, 99
Hole-in-the-Wall 102
Holme Lacy Bridge 94

I

Industrial Revolution, The 165
insects 158
invasive species 154
Irfon, River 168
itineraries, expedition 24, 26

K

kayaks 15
Kerne Bridge 107
King Arthur's Cave 119
kingfisher 158
Kymin, The 124, 125

L

Lady Park Wood 118
Llanelwedd 61
Llangurig 42, 43, 46, 47
Llanstephan Bridge 68
Llanwrthwl Bridge 54
Llewelyn's Cave 63
Locksters Pool 80
Longhope Reach 134
Lower Lydbrook 108, 111

Lower Wye 12, 105
Lucksall Caravan & Camping Park 91, 94
Lugg, River 168
Lydbrook Shallows 111, 112

M

mammals 156
maps 29
Martridge Wood 133
Maze, The 108
Merbach Hill 79
Middle Wye 12, 70
mink 154
Moccas Court 83
Monmouth 115, 121, 123, 124, 126
Monmouth Bridge 121, 125
Monmouth Castle 126
Monnington Falls 86, 87
Monnington-on-Wye 87
Monnow Bridge 126
Mordiford 91, 94
mountain biking 41, 46, 52, 74, 115, 116, 169

N

Nant yr Arian Forest 41
Nelson Museum 126
Newbridge-on-Wye 51, 55, 57
New Weir, Symonds Yat 120

O

Offa's Dyke 87, 127, 130, 165, 168
Ordnance Survey maps 29
otter 157
outdoor activities 168
Owain Glyndŵr 76, 87

P

Penddol Rocks 59
peregrine falcon 113, 159
Peregrine Path Cycle Trail 116, 169
phone, equipment 20
Piercefield Cliffs 133, 134
Piercefield Park 130, 133
planning 15
plants 155
Plynlimon 35, 36, 37
Pont Llangurig 41, 43, 45
Pont Marteg 46, 49
Pont Rhydgaled 35, 39, 41, 42
Port Walls, Chepstow 138
Prince of Wales 64
Public Right of Navigation 143

R

Rebecca Riots 55
Redbrook 126
red kite 41, 159
rescue 22
Rhayader 45, 46, 47, 49, 51, 53
River Festival, Hereford 88
river hazards 20
river levels 12, 22
Rivers Wye and Lugg Navigation Act 87, 165
Roaring Meg 111
Ross-on-Wye 99, 103, 107, 109
Rotherwas Chapel 91, 94
Royal Welsh Showground 61, 62

S

safety 18
salmon 156
sand martin 110, 158
Sellack 101
Seven Sisters Rocks 118
Severn and Wye Expedition Network 28
Severn Area Rescue Association (SARA) 22, 141
Severn Bridge 138, 140
Severn Estuary 137, 139, 140, 141
Silver Mining Museum 41
sit-on-top 15
source of the Wye 35, 37
spawning seasons 170
stand up paddleboards 16
St Briavels Castle 124
St Catherine's Church, Hoarwithy 96, 97, 100
St Curig 43
sterilisation, equipment 154
St Tecla's Island 140
St Twrog's Chapel 140
Sufton Court 91
sun protection 20
SUP 16
Symonds Yat 116
Symonds Yat East 107, 108, 113, 115
Symonds Yat rapids 117, 120
Symonds Yat Rock 108, 113, 115
Symonds Yat West 108, 113

T

Talgarth 67
The Groe 59
Tintern Abbey 130, 131, 132, 133
tourist information 172
Town Falls 47, 49
trees 156

U

Upper Wye 11, 32

V

Voluntary Access Arrangements 144

W

wagtail 159
walking 46, 74, 92, 108, 115, 130, 168
Walking Festival, Ross-on-Wye 103
water levels 12, 22
Waterworks Museum, Hereford 85
Weirend rapid 110
Weir Gardens, The 85, 87
weirs 165
whitewater 26
Whitney Bridge 73, 77, 79, 80
Whitney-on-Wye 79, 80
wild boar 157
wildlife 153, 155
Wilton Bridge 110
Wilton Castle 110
Wintour's Leap 134
Woolhope Dome 92, 94
Wyastone Leys 121
Wyedean Canoe Centre 108, 113, 115, 117
Wye, Lower 12, 105
Wye, Middle 12, 70
Wye, Mouth 137
Wye, River 11
Wyeside Arts Centre 61
Wye, source 35, 37
Wye Tour, The 167
Wye, Upper 11, 32
Wye Valley Area of Outstanding Natural Beauty 94, 153, 154
Wye Valley Canoes 75
Wye Valley Lead Mine 39
Wyndcliff 133, 134

Y

Yat Rock 108, 113, 115

Canoe & Kayak Sales & Hire
Canoe & Kayak Equipment
Outdoor Equipment
Outdoor Clothing

summittosea.co.uk

Unit 10a Penrhos Industrial Estate, Holyhead,
Ynys Mon / Anglesey, LL65 2UQ
e: info@summittosea.co.uk t: +44(0)1407 740963